FOR WHAT IT'S WORTH

*Create a Stronger You,
Rise Above Those Who Don't Understand,
and Build the Life You Deserve*

DENA CHERNENKOFF RN, BSCN

◆ FriesenPress

One Printers Way
Altona, MB R0G 0B0
Canada

www.friesenpress.com

Copyright © 2024 by Dena Chernenkoff, RN, BScN
First Edition — 2024

All rights reserved.

No part of this publication may be reproduced in any form, or by any means, electronic or mechanical, including photocopying, recording, or any information browsing, storage, or retrieval system, without permission in writing from FriesenPress.

ISBN
978-1-03-919485-4 (Hardcover)
978-1-03-919484-7 (Paperback)
978-1-03-919486-1 (eBook)

1. SELF-HELP, PERSONAL GROWTH, SELF-ESTEEM

Distributed to the trade by The Ingram Book Company

You can't control what others do to you, but you can surely control what you do next.

A MESSAGE FROM THE AUTHOR

*I*f you've ever found yourself daydreaming about what life could be like, you've lost something along the way.

Pay attention now, there's hope in that daydream. There's an underlying plan even you don't understand yet.

It's time to do a life inventory. Do you feel happy? Fulfilled with the life you have created? I know, you are grateful for what you have, and you are blessed. But you can be blessed and still have a lot going on. If you feel unsettled in some way, it is because you are not supposed to settle. What is it that you actually want?

If you had to leave tomorrow, and could look back at your life, what would you have changed? Are you proud of the person you are? Are you proud of the parent you are? To be content is to understand your full potential. Are you fulfilled? Or just filling your days because it's too overwhelming to know where to begin.

It's time to start. We want very few regrets. Living your life through the challenges means more than suffering in the unknowing. For what it's worth.

It's time to learn how to actually change all the things that come together and make you whole.

~D

The passion I've had for healing has been for as long as I can remember. If I could help heal that hurt in your heart, it's all worthwhile for me. When you have felt pain, you understand it.

You have no idea what your life could be like, if you're not willing to look in. You are so close to a lasting change. It's time to learn how powerful pain can be. You will see there is beauty in the struggle. The art of your hidden strength.

Are you ready to look in?

photo by First Glance Studios
hair & make-up by Emily Phung Makeup

Contents

PROLOGUE 1

INTRODUCTION. 3

PART 1. UNDERSTANDING HOW YOU GOT HERE 7

    CH 1.   PIG POOP & WHITE FENCES 9

    CH 2.   I DON'T GET IT. 19

    CH 3.   I KNOW I LOST IT SOMEWHERE 25

    CH 4.   SEEING THINGS DIFFERENTLY 39

    CH 5.   ABOUT THOSE PEOPLE 47

    CH 6.   TIME TO BE HONEST 67

    CH 7.   THE JONESES ARE ASSHOLES 71

    CH 8.   HOW TO CHANGE THINGS. 77

    CH 9.   THE THING NOBODY EVER TELLS YOU 89

    CH 10. MY FAVOURITE BATTLE GEAR 105

    CH 11. ADVERSITY AT ITS FINEST. 111

PART 2. BUILDING A BETTER, STRONGER YOU 121

- Ch 12. Getting to Know Your Body 123
- Ch 13. Finding Your Voice 131
- Ch 14. The One Person You Need 145
- Ch 15. Your Body, Your Health 153
- Ch 16. I Think We Should Talk 169
- Ch 17. Get Rich 187
- Ch 18. Money Talks 195
- Ch 19. Complexity in Relationships 209
- Ch 20. Drawing the Lines 231
- Ch 21. A Little Perspective 247
- Ch 22. Superpowers 263
- Ch 23. It's Your Turn 271

*What will you do,
with the power that is you?*

PROLOGUE

There's something so raw about being in duress. The adrenaline from the stress response, like a high taking you away from all of the little things that pass through your brain in a constant stream. Like a rain that clears the cloudy dust, your brain readjusts to focus on what is now. Only one thing to think and do for now. *Survival at its finest.* And like any toxic habit—another drink for the alcoholic, another high for the drug addict—starvation for the person with extreme body dysmorphia—your body wants what it knows best.

Stress is a high. It is a response in your body that creates that focus that takes you away from all the hard stuff that never seems to leave your mind and all of the questions you don't know how to answer, like how can you become what deep inside you know you're meant to be? That overwhelm of what it would take to get there makes it so much easier to ignore, and so we continue to ride the adrenaline wave. Our best-known escape.

Sitting in peace is truly uncomfortable when you have never had the chance to sit in it before. Like losing your virginity, it feels scary and unknown. All firsts are hard, but the excitement makes the hard worthwhile and it always gets easier after a while. Your body finds a new normal. A new thermostat setting that it can run on comfortably. Everybody loves a comfort zone. This one though, is about finding comfort in peace. You are going to be squirming inside, longing to find that adrenaline high again. You'll even start looking for it in other ways because your ego doesn't know how to sit in peace. It wants the high. But your soul is stronger, rest assured.

*"Tough times never last;
but tough people do."*
— Robert Schuller

INTRODUCTION

Making It Make Sense

I have spent my life running on cortisol; I love the high I get from it. The stress of the escape, the exhilaration of reaching the next goal, the next problem to solve, the next mountain to climb. I've always got to be climbing. I guess you could say I was created this way. Sure, when I was a child, I had no choice but to be hyper-aware. When your Daddy likes to drink and can fly off the handle at any moment, you have to be hyper-aware for survival. But what about in adulthood when you are no longer living under scary Daddy's roof? Why does your body still crave the intensity? Why, when you finally reach a place in life where you don't always have to be on your toes, are your peripherals still constantly scanning? Have to make more money in case it runs out, have to achieve another career goal so that I can gain more respect, have to get all the things I set out to do completed each day because unproductivity gets you nowhere. Have to do better, have to be more, have to please the people...

I did one of my final research projects in nursing school on chronic stress and how detrimental it is to your body. Because I finally get it.

You should really be more grateful. "It could always be worse," my mom would say. "There are many people out there that have it a lot worse than you." She's right about that, you know. It could always be worse. But you know what? I am sick of accepting this as good enough. I am sick of teaching our children that you should be grateful that it's not worse. Like, "I know your dad is mean to you honey, but at least he's not beating you. Let's just be sure to be quiet and stay out of his way when he's mad though, to make sure he doesn't start." Some little girls do get beaten, so she was right about that, it could always have been worse. Every day that I escaped his angry wrath I really was grateful to my core. I could handle the name-calling—that was OK. I got used to it and after a while I started believing it, which made it easier to take because I felt I deserved it, so it just became normal. Humans are amazing in that way. We can adjust to our environment for survival. It's instinct. It's proximity principle.

I have a real problem with this now. Life is too short to settle for accepting all that just falls into your lap and letting people write your story for you. It's time to show them out.

Everyone has a story, so how do you become the writer? How do you get that life you see others have? It starts with something very simple. You learn to trust yourself. You learn to rely on yourself. Because at the end of the day, you will be the only one that truly knows you. The work is in figuring out what you want and who you really are.

INTRODUCTION

One thing we know is that in all stages, it's about learning. The thing is, life happens to each of us in different ways at different times, but what we are never told along the way is that we must get very good at taking care of ourselves. Look to those successful few that have paved their path ahead of you. If you ask any of them how they got where they are, I can assure you 100% that they will tell you they learned how to get what they wanted. I don't know one powerful person that has ever said that they rely on other people to take care of them. Period. Does this sound a little negative to you? A negative Nancy preaching about taking care of yourself and relying on nobody? My name isn't Nancy. And life is dark sometimes, so you must learn how to prepare for the storms and how to come out stronger on the other side.

I hate to be the one who honestly admits it, but people can be really annoying sometimes. Along the way, you find all kinds. Of course, there are the kind and loving ones, the humble successful ones, the leaders and mentors, the nurturers and protectors. But no one ever tells you there will be really mean ones, jealous ones, dishonest ones, judgmental ones, superficial ones, and scary ones. You start to learn about those as you stumble across them, and when you do, you can be blindsided and astonished. It takes a lot of life learning to understand people and why they sometimes do the things they do. I'll tell you what, though. If you take the time to read my words ahead, you will learn of a whole new perspective around forgiveness and come to understand that a person's actions are not who they really are deep down.

I'm going to tell you about my life and offer you a perspective that will allow you to turn a new page in the story that is your life. I'm going to talk about people and how they can affect you, and then I'm going to show you how none of it actually needs to matter to you.

When is the last time you did a wellness check? A real one? We are so lost in busy. Busy is all we know, because it's too damn hard to slow down and let the emotions in. Work more, do more, live in overwhelm. Work harder, don't rest, keep piling it on. Let people piss you off, carry on anyway. Well, your life is about change, and the person you see in the mirror is going to look a little different when we're done. The only person that can change your life is you. It's time to build the life you have only dreamed about. It's going to start with building trust in yourself. Trust is not confidence. Confidence comes and goes, but trusting yourself is at a cellular level. It's what sits in the centre of a human being capable of creating change. This time, it's about you. This time, there will be no looking back. You're going to chase your dreams. Sound cliché? We're actually going to chase them. If you're willing.

PART 1

Understanding how you got here

> *"You are today where your thoughts have brought you; you will be tomorrow where your thoughts take you."*
> — James Allen

1.

PIG POOP & WHITE FENCES

Every year when I was a teenager, we opened up the annual Christmas letter from my cousin's family, and every year, we read about all of their accomplishments and perfection in a life built around their pretty-smelling flowers and white picket fence. Another year of honours and awards to hang on the walls and pats on the back from everyone around them. Their two perfect kids couldn't be any more perfect! All of the instruments they learned to play amazed so many people and the family band they played in was ever so special. They made so many precious memories and spent so much family time together all year. A life like no other.

Well, I grew up smelling pig poop and our fence was broken to shit.

What I didn't know then was that people lie about white picket fences. And now, you won't be fooled by them any longer either. Nobody sends out annual Christmas letters anymore, but the same thing is now known as the highlight reel, and you're getting fooled if you get lost in believing it.

One year, my dad wrote an annual letter. After he read it to us, we all just looked at each other and started laughing at how stupid it all sounded. Life in my childhood was anything but perfect. In fact, the stuff he had put in that letter sounded crazy, but at the same time, it was a 100% complete and honest depiction of what had all happened that year. That was the first moment that I wondered if perfect people actually lie, and if life may not always be about pretty-smelling flowers and white picket fences.

But guess what? I actually love the smell of pig poop. It reminds me of how I got to be so powerful.

I imagine you are asking yourself why I am talking about the smell of pig poop. Well, I seriously do like it. Life on a pig farm was not all roses, but it absolutely made me who I am today. And I'm stronger in the aftermath than I ever was (said every warrior ever).

So, what does it mean to have everything you have ever wanted? To feel raw happiness without effort? The thing you may not believe is, you can have it all—and you don't need to rely on anyone else to get you there. The strength inside you to move past all the hurt and all of the people that hurt you is waiting. What you are missing is confidence. The belief in yourself. At some point, someone took your self-worth away, and it's time you get it back, for a person with no self-worth is an unfulfilled soul.

The ego that takes over a soul leaves it lost with no way out. The ego tells us those mean words we hear in our heads: that we are crazy to think we could be something different or stand up to those people that are pushing us down, that we are too ugly or fat or dumb to become what that feeling in our gut thinks we could be, that we are too weak to stand up or too insignificant to lead. Too many of us are living our lives with our egos in the driver's seat. The ego is where envy comes from. It's where negative energy lives and where resentment lies.

It's time to shake things up. It's time to take control of how you want your life to go. It's time to find your strength.

If you have picked up this book, you must have been praying. Praying for answers, praying for purpose, or praying to change your life in some way, even if you don't know where to start. Maybe you want to figure out who you are supposed to be, or better understand why people do the things they do. Or maybe you just want to learn how to become a better you. It can be really hard to understand the difference between the true self of a person from the choices they sometimes make. Life can be confusing at times, and boy can it hurt when the lessons are upon us. But I promise you two things:

1. *Life can get better.*
2. *You don't need anyone* to fix your life for you.

We live in a world of nature versus nurture, where our innate character traits intermix with the culture, people, and environment around us to create who we are. We get lost when we allow our environment and the people around us to take control over the innate qualities of our souls, changing who we are and who we were meant to become.

Selfishness, greed, power, and hatred show up in the faces of so many people around us, and if we're not careful, these can start to create resentment, fear, and anger inside each of us. It is a toxic spread of the dog-eat-dog world. Yuck. I'm so over it. It's time we stop tolerating certain things and start being able to stand on our own.

This book is going to talk about people. All kinds of them. And it's not going to be sugar-coated with me pretending that the behaviours that come out of people don't annoy me. I know I'm not the only one that has had many experiences with all sorts of different personality types, but I have now become one of those people that no longer accepts the ridiculous behaviour of others that believe they are warranted to do or say whatever they want because it makes them feel better. It's time we start holding these people accountable for their words and actions. It's time we start expecting other humans to think about how it might affect others when they speak to other people without respect, or abuse people because they feel like it. If you have ever had anyone treat you poorly, then you know exactly what I'm talking about. You understand how it feels. My intention is to show you that once you stop accepting that behaviour, you will stop feeling helpless in allowing it to continue. You will start to demand respect from people because you truly believe you deserve it. You will stop envying other people because you will understand that they are not as perfect as they may pretend to be. I want to show you how to hold other people accountable for their actions, but I want you to understand that you cannot change anyone but yourself. It's really about loving people where they are at. But it takes a lot of practise.

If there is one thing about me you should know, it is that I do not live my life within the moulds of others around me. I don't always do "normal." I sometimes choose the harder things, because I've learned not to be afraid of them. I've also opened my eyes to the judgment that is around us with all things life, and I am finally able to stand behind my own choices and value systems without feeling self-conscious about them. People can sure be mean sometimes, but I just don't care about their choice to be so anymore.

Independence. Confidence. Trust. I will instill you with everything I have learned because I know you need it, just as I did. This is a book about finding self-worth, especially after someone has hurt you. Believe me when I tell you, you are more worthy than you think you are. I'm going to help you find value in the person you are inside, which will help you to then find value in the person you are on the outside—the face and the body that faces other people in the world every day. We're going to talk about your poker face, for when you want to hide your inner workings, and then we'll talk about your ability to live your life only for yourself and the others you choose to live for. I will teach you how to be dependent only on yourself before you start letting others in and how to live the way you want without care of the judgment you'll find around you. We are going to talk about those mean people and just what to do with them.

All of you reading this have a different story, and so my words will resonate with you in your own personal way. What I want for you after you finish this book is to feel comfortable and confident that who you are will not be dictated by others. I want for you to have the inner workings to create the strength of independence, to confidently stand without needing anything from anyone else. This will be your freedom. Your pride. Your forever peace inside.

I am an ordinary girl, with a very stubborn mentality to create my own happiness. My stubborn desire for complete independence comes from growing up as a child of abuse in a family of alcoholics. This kind of childhood and early adulthood comes with all sorts of trials and tribulations to break the cycle of alcoholism and abuse, and with the grace of God, I was able to break through and find this life I never thought could even exist. A life of true happiness within myself and the people around me. I can promise you that it did not come easy, and it was years of effort, learning, and battle that brought me here today. I mean it when I say it: I have only God to thank for the person I am now. And now I have this relentless desire to reach out and help others, like you, through the dark parts. To let you know that what you believe to be normal, may not be normal at all. I want you to see that there is hope no matter what situation you are in.

When people ask me why I became a nurse, it's a simple answer: to try to help heal people. Isn't that what most people want in their lives? To make a difference somehow so we feel a sense of purpose? Of contribution? What is your sense of purpose in this life? Do you have any idea what it is? Seems like a pretty popular question, doesn't it?

In childhood, we learn about the world around us. In our early years, we learn who we are and how to have fun. Life really revolves around us in our late teens and twenties—we are meeting people, figuring out what we like and don't like, and discovering how different experiences affect us. In our thirties, the walls come down and the world no longer revolves around us. We develop life wisdom and figure out even more who we are, what we love, and what we are willing to and not willing to tolerate. We start studying people on a deeper level and questioning more things. Life seems a lot more serious here and we really start looking for more. If you think of it this way—that our twenties are for the experiences, thirties are for creating our lives, forties are for building them, and fifties are for enjoying all that we have built—then you can get a glimpse of where you're at now and start to head in the direction you want to go. Remember, life happens to each of us in different ways, at different times, and everyone has a story.

One thing I've come to really understand is that we all have inner struggles that we are battling, and pain can become debilitating. The nurse I am in the emergency room can help put your physical self back together, but she can't help you on the emotional level, despite her strong desire to do so. I'll never give up being a nurse because helping people in their most vulnerable state is something my soul is drawn to. But one thing I've really found is that our emotional health is just as important as our physical health because they connect together to make us whole. It's within our emotional health that our soul resides. Our emotional health encompasses who we really are. Holistic nursing is true healing, and we can't remain physically healthy if our mental and emotional health is in turmoil.

You may not take the time to believe this, but you only get one shot at this life. It's time to daydream again. Everyone wants something out of this life, but to actually chase it, you're going to have to start thinking on a deeper level than what most do. Remember what focus brings into your life. I know you have felt that desire before, that need to accomplish that thing you've always wanted, that life you've always wanted to live. There's purpose in dreaming, you know. Some say that what hurts your heart the most is where you're meant to be doing the work. I've spent a good part of my life just running through storms trying to get through to clear skies and sunshine. Some call it survival mode. Some just call it living. I don't agree with that anymore. The power above created us for more than that, but I don't have to tell you that. You already know it. It's just easier to run the day-to-day than to sit down and do the real work. It will be worth it though, that I can promise. The way you think can save you or drown you. People can save you or drown you. It's time to start trusting yourself to take the reins.

People keep saying to me, "I don't know how you did that," and, "I don't know how you survived that and have the mindset you have now," and, "How did you have the strength to become who you are with everything you have been through?" Well, if it helps, I'm a completely normal human soul, I just may be really stubborn... and motivated to get out of the place I was in.

If we can each learn, find peace and understand change, the whole world can change. Now we've come a long way in history, but Lord knows, we still have a long way to go.

You need to find holistic wellness, improve your physical and emotional self, and figure out who your soul is and what it desires. You need to get your self-worth back to how it once was when you were fresh into this world, before people unknowingly destroyed it. You need to become solely reliant on yourself, and find a strength inside of you that you didn't know existed. I want for you to find love and maintain healthy relationships within family, friends, children, and partners. You need to heal from those who have hurt you and walk the path of understanding to connect your past to your future and learn how to build the most powerful strength inside you—one that will get you through anything. It's possible to change your life and fulfill your honest dreams. Be the writer of your own story.

When I first started writing this book, it was meant to be for those troubled souls that had been abused, and it was meant to give them hope and direction to break the cycle. I'll still be working with those souls in a book all their own, but what I realized when I started this one was that it's not just the abused souls that need help.

We all have past hurt in some way, on some level, and we happen to be living in a world where people are mean. Some of us feel judged, some of us have been bullied, some of us have been talked over and pushed around, some of us have been gossiped about, and some of us have been made to feel that we can't accomplish what we want. All of these experiences diminish our self-worth, and it's time we take it back.

I'm going to be blatantly honest about what I think of people that say or do mean things, but it will not be with the intent to personally attack each of those people. What I say comes with the understanding that they too have stories that have changed them, and it is through that unknowing (or in some cases knowing and just not caring) that they project these negative acts and comments that affect the self-worth of others today. I'm going to try to help you understand how to not let any of them affect you anymore.

To all of you passive people out there, there is hope for you, I promise. Let's empower you, help you understand the human mind from a different perspective, help you become completely independent from needing anyone to survive, and then even better, to thrive. Let's get you everything you have ever wanted, and for some, help you figure out what it is you actually want. This book is about purpose and figuring out what yours is, how to better understand a world that we don't pay enough attention to, how to deal with people, how to heal from the past, and how to reach your dreams.

Now the tricky thing about any task that involves letting go of your past, learning complete independence, dealing with how other people have affected you, and figuring out who you actually are is that we all have lives to work around while we do it. So, it will not be easy, but nothing really good ever is. You will just need to find moments to soul search and find the drive deep inside of you. I promise you, it will be worth it in every way.

"Do the best you can until you know better. Then when you know better, do better."
— Maya Angelou

2.

I DON'T GET IT

"Choose joy."

I really hate when people say that. Oh OK, I'll just forget all my troubles, forget the people that have been mean to me, forget about this pain, and "choose joy." I'll just choose to feel happy because that's what people keep telling me to do. Like it is that easy. I find that everywhere you go, you hear things like, "Live life to the fullest!", "Stop comparing yourself to others!", and "Stop caring what people think!" Ha. Again, like it's that easy.

Most everyone that hears those words has no idea how to actually do those things. Because it's not easy. Or, it's easier said than done, anyway. After you finish this chapter, I have a feeling that you will have a better understanding of how to tackle those attempts with a little more intention and a lot less confusion.

Life is crazy sometimes. You're just living life, making decisions as they come, and trying to figure out what it is you are actually supposed to be doing. Have you ever stopped and thought, how did I even get here? I think one of the hardest parts about figuring out our own lives is that everyone has a different story, so you can start comparing yourself to others when really, we are all walking down individual paths with our own dreams and challenges.

Speaking of our own paths, how are we supposed to find the answer to the question we all eventually ask ourselves: What is our purpose in life? We often feel stuck because we don't really know what we want to do with our lives. And for those of us that have been hurt, how can we move past the hurt and find purpose? How do we figure out who we actually are, and how do we learn to love ourselves? Especially when there are so many people and stories to compare to, and especially when people can sure be mean, how do we accomplish these things?

When I was younger, I used to look at people in awe. They amazed me. Some of them even seemed like gods to me. Superhuman. They were doctors and nurses, teachers and parents, presidents and prime ministers. When your soul is young, you don't understand that these people are just people. Humans, like you.

People say all the time that you can be whatever you want to be. I do believe you can become anyone you want to be, but I think it comes with stipulations that nobody ever really points out. Sure, presidents are normal people that followed a dream they had. The thing we misunderstand is that you can be anything you want to be, but you really have to *want* to be it. So, for example, I think it would be super cool to be the president of a country. You could hold the power to make significant changes to try and improve the quality of living for people. I don't want to be a president enough to want to chase that dream, because the complexities of the policies and procedures involved in politics are not my greatest passion. I know I'm built to become something else.

I like to think that we all have many pre-set paths we can take, and when we get to a crossroads, we have to make a choice. Most of us, I want to say, live in reaction. We live in a story where the choices we make are not so much intentional as they are a reaction to the things and people that happen to us along the way. Once we figure this out, the story of our lives can take a whole new turn. We can start to intentionally think about the things we want to accomplish and the person we want to be. Most of us are never taught this, and so we just keep floating along making reactionary choices that are not directed toward a proper end goal. Have you ever thought about that?

Sometimes I think we go through life wondering who we actually are and what makes us different from everyone else. We ask ourselves, "What's so special about me?" We might think, "I'm just another human on this earth trying to be a good person and live a successful life." But what we are missing is that we *are* special. Sounds fluffy, I know, but we really are each born with something that is unique, and we all have the ability to change the world somehow, through big ways and small. The problem is, we spend most of our lives being taught that we don't matter. We might be hurt by someone we love, put down by strangers that don't even know us, judged by people around us, or let down by somebody we thought we could depend on. This is a big problem, because losing our self-worth through these experiences causes us to lose our fire, our strength, and the power that lives within us.

Most of us feel unworthy. Devalued. We're just another person on the planet, trying to get by with an ordinary plan because we don't feel we are worth anything more. Some of us are trying to understand why people have hurt us so badly. Some of us aren't actually sure we deserve any better.

One of the greatest lessons we should all keep in the back of our minds is that we cannot rely on anyone else. It sounds so dark, doesn't it? It is dark, but if you have ever experienced true hardship, you know exactly what I'm talking about. The biggest learning lesson in life is that you cannot change or control other people's actions. This is why I say that you cannot rely on anyone else but yourself, because you have no control over how someone will react to their life events. Life is hard sometimes, and big things happen that cause us to think or act in ways we might never have expected. The amazing thing is that once you figure out how strong and resilient you are, there's more light that shines through than you could ever have imagined seeing before. It's amazing, actually. It's beautiful. Once you develop that strength, you'll see how powerful you become in clearing the path you were meant to walk. I know, I know, it sounds like the cliché expressions you hear all the time when people say, "Let the light shine in! Change your life!" I used to think, how the hell am I supposed to do that? Let what light shine in? It can be so confusing and annoying to listen to that fluff. But hear me out. I know what I'm talking about here, and you are going to have to get a little bit of a hippy attitude for some of this, as nothing big comes from the everyday earth stuff. You have to think about the world that we can't see. Open your mind to God, the spirt world where your soul came from, and the bigger picture for what your life is supposed to look like.

Let's talk about hiking for a minute. I love exploring nature through new places I've never been and seeing what kind of adventure may lie in quiet areas that not many people have been through. Fresh air, warm sunshine or crisp winter breaths, clambering up a rocky hill or trudging through fresh snow, watching animals in their own worlds. Hiking through older forests, you have to clear all the deadfall and overrun branches from your path, otherwise they slow you down. As you work on clearing, you eventually start seeing a path form, the sun shines through, and you start moving a little faster. After a lot of work, you just start strolling and life feels a whole lot easier. It's the same for the work I am talking about for reclaiming your self-worth and discovering your life's path. I promise you it's worth it.

For some of us, God needs to spread a forest fire to clear out the deadfall because it's just too thick for us to be able to figure out where to even start for ourselves. But the purpose of the forest fire is to clear everything and allow for new growth. Have you ever seen a forest rebuild itself after destruction? It's incredible. My husband was raised in the mountains, and every year he takes me for a drive through the terrain. The first time he showed me the destruction of a fire and the beauty that grew up after it, it all just made sense. New growth shows up almost immediately after the fire is out. The energy is peaceful and new life is all around. Animals come back and create new homes, the sun is able to reach through and start touching the new plant life, and life becomes full in the forest again. Full and fresh. This is exactly what happens after the storms in our lives. We come out changed and stronger. The deadfall is burnt away and we smile and walk ahead with new-found peace and gratitude. Contentment at its finest. Healthy relationships start to form around us and create a life within our circle, and we stand independent and strong, surrounded by love.

If you think you are too small to make a difference, try sleeping with a mosquito.
— Dalai Lama

3.

I KNOW I LOST IT SOMEWHERE

We are not born thinking we are unworthy. Babies come into this world with complete trust for others around them because they are completely dependent on other people to survive. Young kids don't wonder if they are good enough until they reach an age where comparison sets in. They say the first five years of attachment are imperative for children to develop trust and the feeling of being loved. I would absolutely agree with this statement, except it doesn't stop there. Most of our lives are spent learning about trust and love and everyone needs someone in their lives to show them just how important and valuable they are. The problem is that most of us do not have that person, which is evidenced by those with stable childhoods who still have ongoing trust and self-worth issues.

These issues develop from the negative impact of actions and words of other people throughout their lives. They might have had someone tell them they were loved, but they may also have heard the opposite at times, and believing the negative things we hear is usually easier than believing the positive. So, we need to start young and we need to stay consistent in preaching to all young, developing people how very worthy they are.

Think back to your childhood. What were the defining moments in your life where you remember realizing that you were not as special as you thought you were? Was someone mean to you? Did they call you names or tease you? Did someone you loved hurt you or make you feel like you were not worthy of their love? Are there any memories that come up, even vaguely, that remind you of a time you felt embarrassed or hurt from someone's words or an event that happened? Were you at home or at school? Maybe at a sporting event? It may even be as light as being cut from team tryouts or a comment a teacher or coach made that embarrassed you. It could have been a rejection from a crush you had or gossip that someone spread about you. Whatever it was, it is in these moments that our self-worth begins to dwindle. This happens in our younger years and carries into our teenage years and our twenties. For most of us, it continues to carry through into our thirties and forties if we don't recognize it and stop it. It can have a great impact on the expectations we hold of ourselves and how we let others treat us.

The work we have to do today to clear that toxicity from inside of us starts with recognition. Once you recognize the person and the words that hurt you and are honest about how it made you feel, I want you to sit on it for a while and reflect on how it has impacted the way you make decisions today. I want you to ask yourself if you truly believe whatever was said about you is true. Hear the answer that first arises within you: a yes or a no.

If the answer is no, then you are closer to self-worth than you thought. If it is yes, then we have a lot more work to do.

One day when I was five, I was sitting at the table eating breakfast. We were pig farmers, so my mom always made us bacon and eggs every morning. My dad was glaring at me from his seat at the head of the table. It looked like he wanted to hurt me. I didn't know he was looking at me like that, so I continued to nervously eat my breakfast and tried not to look directly at him. Finally, my mom whispered in my ear, "Honey, chew with your mouth closed." I hadn't realized until then that I was making sounds while I ate. I immediately made a conscious effort to keep my lips sealed after every bite. My brothers were seated across the table. Nobody spoke. My dad looked away from me but continued to glance up and glare at me every few seconds. I decided then that maybe I shouldn't continue my breakfast in case I was still making too much noise and angering him. I left the table, finished getting my stuff ready for school, and headed out to the end of the laneway early to wait for the bus.

Later on, at school, my teacher asked me why I wasn't eating my lunch. I told her I wasn't hungry. I don't honestly remember if I was hungry or not, I just remember not wanting to eat. I was too young to understand any further; I just knew that I didn't want to eat. A week later, my teacher called my mom in for a meeting. I listened to her express her concern about how I had not eaten at school every day for the past week. She was worried and wanted to know if my mom knew of any reason why this might be. My mom said she didn't know, but on the drive home, she told me that even though the lip smacking sounds my mouth made when I ate made my dad really mad, it was OK to eat at school, just as long as I remembered to keep my mouth closed.

Even after this talk, I still remember not being hungry. Just scared inside. And I remember feeling at that time that it was much better to avoid doing the thing that would cause someone to hate me than it would be to do it, even if it benefited me. Every meal time that I was forced to sit at the table with my family after that was never relaxing. I always made sure not to speak too much, only answer when I was asked something, and for God's sake keep my mouth closed when I chewed.

As time passed and I grew a little older, I got better at understanding that it was normal for my dad to glare at me from across the room with a look of sheer hate some days. I never knew why he did it. I would just be doing something in the kitchen or he would catch sight of me from his spot at the table at start glaring. Maybe he hated the sound of my voice? Maybe I made him mad by just being alive? I wasn't sure, but either way, I learned to ignore it and stay out of his way.

He glared at my mother a lot too, so I figured he just didn't like us because we were girls. He called my mom "big buck" and I was "little buck." These were short for "big buckin' fitch" and "little buckin' fitch," because he said he couldn't call us the real words in public. Eventually, they were shortened. I don't know why my brothers never got names, but I learned that this was just how it was, and that was what he called us. It became my normal. I knew I was hated for being myself at home, so I learned quickly to adapt myself around other people so that I hopefully wouldn't make them mad for being myself as well. I wasn't ever sure what about me made people so mad, I just knew I didn't want the whole world to hate me, so I started doing whatever I could to please people. All people. I learned how to act how they wanted me to act, like what they liked, talk when I thought it was allowed or accepted, and adapt to the environment around me. And that is how people pleasers are created.

That little blond girl I think about now breaks my heart. If I could go back in time and hold her and tell her just how special she really is, I would. The funny thing about kids is they just don't know any different, so they adapt. I watched my dad treat my mother the same way he treated me, and I figured that she didn't think I was special or loved in any way because she wasn't either. That's just how it was. Boys were treated a little less harshly, while girls were just lucky to not be hit. My brothers did know that it wasn't an option to misbehave though. If they were ever in trouble, most times it wasn't just a light talking-to.

I remember the day my little brother was sent to the principle's office at school. When we all got home, I watched my dad lift him a foot off the ground in a choke hold, one hand around his throat, staring a death stare into his scared little blue eyes. My brother was fourteen. My mom made sure to keep the rest of us quiet and out of my dad's way. That was her way of protecting us.

I am a mother of three now, soon to be four as I write this book. I have two boys and one girl, and I hug them all today the way I wish I could have been hugged when I was young.

My daughter is seven now, and when I look at her, I sometimes think of my little blond self when I was her age. I know now that all children deserve to be loved unconditionally, because when they aren't, they grown up believing that they are unworthy of love or happiness. This toxic mindset then spreads to their children and spouses, until we have what we have today, in the twenty-first century. Too many children are hurt every day by this toxic cycle. Kids take a lot of patience to deal with, as all of you that are parents have come to learn very quickly, but they still all deserve unconditional love.

Humans are slow learners, but it's time we look to a higher power to understand how we are truly built and what it is He actually wants for us. He wants for us to be kind to one another.

To love and accept one another. To cherish our children. To help our neighbours. It's really that simple. So why is it so hard?

If you are a people pleaser, the trait is a combination of your passive personality from nature (the character and personality of the person you inherently are) and the learned habits and actions from nurture (the experiences you have been exposed to).

To further break these concepts down, the nature of a person is their natural personality—some of us are more sensitive than others, or more emotional, logical, loud, quiet, calm, restless, or aggressive in nature. The nurture aspect of a person is how they react to their experiences, environment, and the people in their lives.

If you are a people pleaser, you try to find self-worth in pleasing others. Making them feel comfortable and happy with your actions prevents you from feeling shame or rejection. You search for worth in the external approval of others. This behaviour stems from a combination of our natural personality, our level of sensitivity, and our past traumas, big or small. When we are affected by trauma, it affects our self-worth.

My husband tells me that people will push you around if you let them. The more passive you are, the more they will take advantage of you. I just couldn't wrap my head around this at first. Why would people be mean to someone who is kind and submissive? I just didn't understand it, and so it just kept happening—to me. Everywhere I went, I allowed people to treat me however they wanted to treat me, including poorly. I think for some, treating me this way somehow made them feel better. It may have helped them release built-up anger, frustration, or sadness. In this way, us passive folks become the fixers for these people. We fix them by allowing their bad behaviour to be directed at us, making them feel better. Put your hands up all of you fixers, you know who you are.

As for those people that take their frustrations out on you? Think about emotional regulation and unconditional love. It is easier to be rude to someone that you know loves you very much—like a spouse, parent, sibling, or child—than it is to be rude to anyone else—like a work colleague, friend, or child's coach. It is easier to release frustration on someone when you know they will still love you afterward, whereas you may not act a certain way or say certain words to someone you think might not tolerate it for fear of judgment or repercussion.

For example, you might not voice anger toward your child's coach for fear that your child might lose playing time as a result. Or, maybe you would be scared that people would gossip about you or you could be fired if you had an outburst at a colleague at work. Likewise, an abuser might be taken to the authorities if people found out they hurt their child on a regular basis, so they learn to control their temper in certain situations, then let the child have it when they are alone in their house behind walls that don't talk. The point here is that we all have control over our actions.

For some, they don't worry about judgment and choose to act out at strangers, work colleagues, or whoever else crosses their path and makes them mad. If that happens to be you and you are passive and submissive, then you are giving them permission to treat you poorly. For me, this happened everywhere around me. The bank teller, the guy walking his dog that didn't like that my dog barked at his dog, my angry and bitter nurse colleagues, a large portion of my patient population, my father, my superficial friends that gossip and judge, the irritated store clerk, or the lippy girl at the registry office. The list goes on. And

I just wasn't understanding why they were all around me, and why I deserved it.

What I didn't understand all along is that it was never about me. People are going to treat you the way that you allow them to. That was my life lesson. My husband used to say, "It sure is funny how all these people say this crap to you when I'm not around," and that is exactly why they would say it: because he wasn't around. If he were around, he would never have allowed it. He's strong, vocal, and takes no crap from anyone anymore after years of working on construction sites with angry, bitter, divorced, discontent, and stressed men that had nothing to be happy about. In that environment, he quickly learned what people can be like if you allow them to get away with it.

The reason I now know why people kept treating me badly was because I wasn't understanding the learning lesson in it. Here's the thing about life lessons: if you don't catch on, the lesson just keeps coming until you get hit over the head with it. So, wake up now to the patterns in your life and figure out what lessons for your soul are in them. Or else they will just keep repeating themselves.

Light bulb moments are when a light suddenly flicks on in your mind and you understand something from a whole new perspective. Maybe for some of you it feels more like a hammer hitting you on the head. I love light bulb moments. They are so helpful for growth and development, and every time you figure out something true to you, a new path appears for you to walk, leading you in the direction you are meant to be headed in your life, and you are saved from making the same mistakes again, saving you from a lot of unnecessary frustration and heartache. One of my most important light bulb moments was understanding that the way people treat you has nothing to do with the value of the person you are, but rather with the tolerances you hold to their actions toward you. Passive people get stepped on more because they allow it. Simple, but hard to understand until you experience practising boundaries and asserting yourself when it comes to what behaviour you will accept. Once you realize you are allowing bad behaviour and you take steps to stop doing so, people will start treating you differently.

We must work on developing self-worth through internal work, and this is where this book was born. I know that I'm not the only passive people pleaser out there who didn't believe they were worthy of being treated properly. We cannot find true confidence and happiness in ourselves if we do not believe we are worthy.

I am going to tell you a story about the little girl in me learning what it meant to feel sad and unsure. You too were once born innocently into this world, and maybe my story will help you think about your own younger self, so that you can start to unpack emotions that need to be validated. You have to start somewhere to be able to change the way you think about yourself and get your confidence back. You might have lost it so long ago that you don't remember what it feels like to have it. Well let me tell you, it is very much worth the unpacking, as hard as it will be. Just remember that everyone has a different story, with different experiences that affect them in unique ways. What affected you might not affect another person the same way. Try to understand that it's all relative here, and your reflections are yours alone.

My story begins on a particular afternoon at my grandma's house when I was five years old. It was my first ever experience with humiliation, confusion, and true loneliness. It was one of those moments in life where I was left changed, even though I didn't fully understand why or how.

We lived a mile from my grandma and grandpa growing up, so it was my home away from home. My grandma and grandpa were people of gold; they were so kind and sweet, hardworking and loving. I remember having so much fun playing in their yard with my cousins and camping and fishing. One thing was for sure though: we were always taught not to discuss much about emotions.

My grandpa was a tough old farmer and my grandma, well, she had quite the story, that's for sure. She was one of those quiet-about-her-past kinds of people, the ones that hold their chin up and look so put together all the time. Her hair was always done, nails painted, and clothes classically elegant. Her lips, though perfectly rouge coloured, were always pursed. Very rarely did I ever notice her look relaxed in her body posture. She always held herself with strength.

My grandma's father was a very mean man. He was an alcoholic—the kind that you hid from when he was mad—and he was mad for most of her childhood. My grandma used to have to hide all her siblings in dresser drawers while their father beat their mother in the kitchen. She would have to hunt gofers to feed her siblings while her mother recovered from his beatings, and he would sometimes disappear for months on end while his family starved at home.

My father followed a little in his grandfather's footsteps. He too was an abusive alcoholic, however the stories I had heard about what happened to my grandma never happened to me. My family lost my little brother in a quad accident when he was fifteen years old, and my father and mother did not cope well after. Alcoholism is a crazy disease. It's amazing what people will put themselves through to numb their pain. Considering that the stories about how my grandma was abused was what I had to compare to, I always thought that what my dad did wasn't that bad. I mean, wasn't it normal to be yelled at, hit, spanked, and called names? I thought he was just stressed, trying to make a living and feed his family. Nobody ever had to hide me in a dresser drawer anyway, mind you looking back now, I sure wish someone would have.

My mother and my grandmother lived by burying all of their trauma and the destruction of their self-worth deep within their souls. Deep enough to be able to cope day to day and not have to relive it, or even think about it. So that's what they taught me to do too. You were not supposed to speak of it. Things just were how they were and we just had to learn to toughen up and deal with it. My mom used to say, "Suck it up, princess," and my grandma, "Wipe your tears, the men are coming in." And that is how I became so strong on the outside... and how loneliness started to form on the inside and my self-worth began dwindling away.

Returning to my story, when I was little, I had an invisible friend I called Jennifer. She was the size of a Barbie and her hair was long and blond like mine, but hers reached all the way down to the small of her back. She was so calm and gentle and kind. Her eyes were soft and blue. The day she showed up, I had been playing with Barbies in my room. It was loud outside my walls, scary and with lots of yelling, again. I felt so scared so often, but when she came that day, I felt safe for the first time that I could remember. I was so relieved. Like whatever was squeezing my heart so much finally let go, and I could breathe again. She stayed and played with me. We put Barbie and Ken in Barbie's pink car with the top down. We dressed Barbie's friends in beautiful dresses and changed their shoes. The Barbies laughed and Ken was so nice to them all. We played for hours I think—time just seemed to stand still. I felt so happy. I wasn't so lonely anymore. After that, Jennifer showed up every day. She often sat or stood on my right shoulder, especially as I walked around the house. Whenever she was there, I knew I wasn't alone. I knew I would be OK.

So that one afternoon at my grandma's, my cousins had come down to visit. I had been talking to Jennifer, only to look up at my older cousin and see that he was laughing at me. I felt the warmth in my chest and my neck rising up to fill my cheeks. He had seen me talking to my invisible friend. Humiliation filled my insides. The laughter spread to my other cousins. Was Jennifer not real? Why could I see her then? Why could I hear her voice when she told me it was OK and that I would be alright? I was torn between the embarrassment of being laughed at and the shock of the sudden realization that the little person that made me feel safe didn't exist. There was a whirlwind of thoughts and emotions suddenly swirling around my mind: *I can't let them see me get upset. They're all staring at me now.* I quickly stood up and walked into the living room, away from all those eyes. I needed to process what had happened. I needed to hide. I spent the rest of that afternoon trying to wrap my head around the fact that Jennifer wasn't real. My heart was broken. I felt so lonely again, and unsure. I missed her already. I never forgot how embarrassed I felt that day. And Jennifer never came back.

When I look back at little blond me, sitting in her bedroom, my heart aches for her. The day I saw this girl, little me, was the day I started to gain back my self-worth. I believe in the spirit world and I believe in God, guardian angels, and spirit guides. Was Jennifer a figment of my imagination? Or was she sent from above to soothe the soul of a frightened little girl in a troubled home? When I was made to feel embarrassed, she disappeared, so maybe my mind no longer allowed me to let anyone in.

Everyone has the ability to feel the spirit world if they are open to it. I strongly urge you to quiet down and start listening. When

I KNOW I LOST IT SOMEWHERE

I look at my beautiful daughter, I can see she is as innocent and sweet as I was, and I finally realize that everyone is born innocent, sent as a spirit from our higher power. From there, our nature—who we were designed to be—and our nurture—what our environment and culture does to help form us—creates our own unique story. We all have different life experiences, and the growth of our soul through our individual learning process is what the whole purpose of human nature is.

The physical body, the mind, and the soul all connect to make us whole, but it is within the soul that our purpose lies. It is who we really are. As soon as you come into this world, the learning starts. We spend our whole lives building our character and developing our souls. It has been said that our souls choose our parents and our life happenings before we are sent to earth to learn our intended lessons and develop our souls. Some people have faith in the spirit world with an understanding that there is a higher power and a bigger picture. Some have faith in a religious structure, where the higher power of God communicates through the bible and stories of humans learning throughout history. If we read the bible and listen to our souls, we'll find connections and feelings as to what our higher power intended for us to become that ring true to our hearts.

I come from a Christian background. Religion is a beautiful thing, until humans start to perceive the bible in different ways, causing hatred and war. Many religions have been started by people creating their own version of the bible and forming their own rules. One thing I know to be true in what seems to be a complex mess of people's varying belief systems, faiths, upbringings, and cultures is that the higher power of God that created this earth holds each one of us dear to his heart.

Being kind to one another is one of God's main desires for the human race. But when we are given free choice, the ego can sometimes take over the soul of the person we truly are. From there, we lose our self-worth when other humans are mean to us. As you now know, I lost mine when I was just little.

The stories of people being mean, judgmental, and critical will not stop until every person begins to find their soul. We've come a long way in history, but we still have a long way to go.

Beneath your debilitating pain lies the beginning of your healing, your self-worth, and your soul filled with peace. It is through healing that you will learn you need only to rely on yourself, build trust in yourself, and be your only saviour. No longer will you live your life conforming to other people's opinions. No longer will you tolerate other people hurting you.

As I've said before, everyone has a story. You are the only writer of yours. It's time to hear your soul and to start living your life the way it was meant to be lived. Here you will learn to find a strength you never knew existed, and you will lean on only those around you that genuinely love you. You will learn what acceptable behaviour is, and it will align with the values and belief systems that you develop for yourself (not that you just follow from others). You will learn to develop your own boundaries to protect your soul.

It is time to quiet down the ego of the mind and find your self-worth again. You once had it—it's just been clouded over with life's happenings and the people that have happened to you.

> *"A wise woman wishes to be no one's enemy; a wise woman refuses to be anyone's victim."*
> — Maya Angelou

4.

SEEING THINGS DIFFERENTLY

There's a lot of different advice out there about mean people. You might hear that if someone treats you poorly then they never really loved you, or if someone is mean then they deserve to be punished. At points in our lives when we feel most angry at someone, it can be really easy to think these things. That's a fact, I don't care who you are. But after years of dealing with abuse in my younger days, and coming across all kinds of people in my older adult years, I have found a new way of looking at things. Maybe it's all the Dalai Lama books I've read, or the innate forgiving nature I seem to have been born with, but whatever it is, you need to listen: Anger and resentment do nothing for your internal health. At all. They also do nothing to the person that has mistreated you. I hate to break it to you, but that person doesn't care how they've affected you. They are too lost in their own little world of hurt, anger, negativity, shame, and sadness to be concerned by how you are doing after they were mean to you. They don't care now, and they never will. But it's not because they don't love you, or they never loved you, or they hate you. It's got nothing to do with you. It's only about them; you just happened to be in their way.

If you watch the patterns, you'll know that those who are mean are mean to more than just you. Because again, it's not about you. Unless, of course, you have been antagonizing them or have done something horrible to them, causing them to lash out at you. That's a different story from what I am talking about here, which is you just living your life, trying your best, and coming across people that are mean to you. On all levels. This includes being verbally or physically abusive, judgmental, or disrespectful toward you. It includes gossiping about you, throwing you under the bus, allowing you to take the fall for something you didn't do, blaming you, lying to you, or manipulating you.

Here's what you need to know:

1. *It is not about you.* Everyone is on their own learning journey and you are just a part of that mean person's learning. Everyone is struggling with their own internal battles, and you are not the centre of their world. You are just there.

2. *Letting go* of the things people have said or done to hurt you and forgiving them is one of the hardest things you'll ever have to do in your life. We'll tackle this in the chapter on forgiveness, but know right now that it

is essential in order to move forward in the process of living your own life for you.

3. *Creating boundaries* and knowing when to let people go from your life will be the most life-changing lesson you will learn. We'll go over this later in the book. You will feel the biggest weight lift off your shoulders and it will change who you are.

4. *Gratitude is the base for all healing.* Everything you learn will be taken back to gratitude. The ability to feel grateful is what separates those of us who trudge through life from those of us who soar. It separates those that cannot cope from those that win their battles. Gratitude is one of the secret powers you'll learn to develop to make you stronger than you ever thought possible. It will set you free.

5. *Perspective is huge.* Once we have the ability to change the way we look at something or someone, it sets us free from all of the hurt, resentment, and "poor me" mentality that lives within us. It allows us to feel content by doing nothing but changing the way we think. We'll be talking more about perspective, but for now I want you to focus on combining perspective with gratitude. This is about you being hurt and learning a lesson from it. Focus on seeing your hurt through a different lens and finding gratitude in the brokenness you feel. The people that hurt you the most are your best teachers, so let's try to change the way you think about the people who have hurt you. You can be grateful that the meanness of these people has little to do with you and is more about how they are on a very hard learning journey full of shame and confusion. You will learn that your inner strength is

stronger than what anyone can say or do to you because you are one with your soul. Your perspective of your maltreatment will become your strongest power in your ability to overcome it.

Let me tell you a story about the power of a daddy's love. It's about a moment that changed me. A moment I watched happen that created a feeling that overwhelmed my heart, my soul. Suddenly I understood. After a life of so much confusion, so much pain, there it was. I watched before my eyes what love really looked like. I see it more now that I recognize what it is, but the first time I truly understood, it was like God placing it right before my eyes and my heart. That night, I saw where self-worth begins and how it grows.

It was New Year's Eve and Ty, my oldest son, and his buddies were going to a party. They were sixteen years old, and this party was going to be awesome. They were in the kitchen of our house, planning out the night and telling me all about the people who would be at the party and how much fun they were going to have.

One of Ty's buddies eventually spoke up and said, "I'm going to break up with Emma before the party!"

"WHAT!" I responded. "Don't you do that to that poor girl right before a New Year's party. What is going on with you guys that makes you feel it's time to end things right now?"

He explained that he felt like he needed to have space to breathe and to not be attached to anyone, that he just wanted to have fun at the party and do what he wanted to do. I explained that it would not be nice to hurt Emma right before a big party, and that having her attend alone and watch him dance with or kiss another girl would break her heart even more. I explained to this group of boys in my kitchen that there was a time and a place to discuss things, and I urged them not to be dismissive of other people's feelings. They of course were all just giggling at the drama of it all and only heard blah blah blah. They carried on downstairs, laughing and having fun.

Ty was dating Emma's sister Olivia at the time, so the girls would be coming over after the party was over. My heart hurt for Emma as I knew in advance what the end of her night would look like.

At one in the morning, the designated drivers began dropping the kids off in groups. When the boys got home, they were laughing and talking about all the fun they'd had. Soon after, Emma and Olivia showed up. Now, you can imagine Miss Emma was not in the best of shape. She had tried to have fun, but seeing the boy who'd broken up with her had caused the tears to stream and she'd had multiple drinks. She couldn't walk a straight line and her heart was a mess. Her long blond hair was disheveled and her beautiful slim body was hunched over. She and Olivia headed straight to the bathroom, where I could hear Emma sobbing while her younger sister tried to console her.

I knocked on the door, and as I entered, Emma looked up at me with light blue, water-filled eyes, her cheeks flushed pink from crying and tears streaming down her face. Memories flooded my heart. I remembered exactly what it had felt like when I was her age and I had found out my boyfriend had cheated on me. You don't forget emotions that strong. It is an experience that leads to more self-worth dwindling away, leaving you to believe that you are not good enough to be with that guy, that something about you is not worth loving. You are left confused and you start to believe that you are not pretty enough or skinny enough or smart enough or funny enough. It feels like there is nothing you can do to change and you are stuck being this person that just isn't worthy. The tears mark defeat and sadness, heartache and destruction. And at this age, when you are already unsure of who you are and who you should be, those emotions ride strong. You don't understand that these feelings of despair will pass—it just feels like your life is over right then and there.

As I rubbed Emma's back, she looked at me with her glossy eyes and asked, "what's wrong with me? Why did he let me go, just like that?"

As I stared into this sweet girl's soul, I just kept flashing back to all my heartaches from my teen years. The boyfriends that cheated and my daddy who was not nice to me.

I looked deep into her eyes and said, "One day, girl, you will look in the mirror and actually see how beautiful you are, inside and out. One day, you'll feel like you matter. But right now, you have no idea. You have no idea how beautiful you are, how smart and fun you are, how much you mean to people, or how beautiful your soul is. One day you'll see it. One day you will feel worthy."

I phoned Emma's parents and spoke with her mom. I made sure she knew she was safe but had had a tough night. I was told her dad was on his way.

Her dad was a tall, wide-shouldered man who was the school principal in town. He walked with a strong, gruff stride up to the door. He was not happy with his daughters. They had left him worried and they had drunk too much. As he sternly started in on Emma, asking her what she was thinking, I quietly said to him, "She has had a tough night. Her heart is broken. Go easy on her."

In that moment, his whole demeanour changed. He looked into her soul with an immediately protective love. His face softened, and as he wrapped his jacket around her, he brought her into his safe arms.

SEEING THINGS DIFFERENTLY

"OK, Emma, let's go home," he said as she melted into his chest. She was sobbing, and he held her.

That was the moment I would never forget. His love for her was so strong that I felt it in my heart. I have never felt so grateful to witness something so powerful. The power of a daddy's love for his daughter. And in that moment, I knew she was going to be OK. Tears filled my eyes as he picked her up and softly placed her in the passenger seat of his car. I thanked God that night for letting me be present to witness this, to place before me this love.

Olivia made her way out to the car as well with Ty supporting her arm. She was telling her dad how she didn't do anything she wasn't supposed to, pretending to be innocent just as younger sisters do sometimes. Her dad wasn't buying it. She happily made her way to the truck, where Ty helped her into the back and shook her father's hand.

As they drove away, my heart felt full. I smiled at my boy, proud and full of love. We walked back into the house and I said goodnight to him and the few kids left that were sleeping over. I'll always be grateful for that night.

You can see how we get lost in life happenings sometimes. They can make us start looking at ourselves the way others do—with judgment or in a way that puts us down. As I said earlier, the thing we need to understand is that the judgment or heartbreak, pain or anger toward us from others is hardly ever about us in the first place. Everyone has a story, and everyone carries emotions that reflect the thoughts and feelings they have about the experiences they are going through on their own life paths. The only way we find our own self-worth again is by giving ourselves grace and forgiving ourselves for what we did not know about others. Each experience brings a new awareness, but only those of us who are open to recognizing when lessons are being handed to us will build character and change the way we see ourselves and the way we make choices in our lives.

The lesson I learned that New Year's Eve was that I am no different than Emma, and neither are you. The beauty I saw in her and the love she was worthy of from her dad, is no different than my own beauty and worth, or yours. I just don't have the same story, and neither do you.

Your life isn't about all the people that have hurt you. It is about how you react to them and how you learn to value yourself. You must not rely on other people in order to form your opinion of yourself. For this you must quiet down and listen to your soul. Recognize your strengths and see what makes you different from others. You will naturally look to other people for validation and it's okay to take compliments as they come, and to take criticism with an open mind. You might need to work on improving your reaction to criticism, or you might need to learn that criticism can be a veil for someone who is spewing judgment and reflections of the qualities they don't like in themselves onto you.

When people are mean, it is a direct reflection of their own insecurities and pain. You must begin to recognize this in people and in their comments, and look within to ask yourself if what's being said is really true. If you listen, your soul will speak to you. It has all the answers to who you really are inside, and it will guide you toward the purpose and path you were set here to walk down. The closer you connect with your soul, the more you will find self-worth and gain confidence in knowing who you are. You deserve love and happiness, and you need to understand that you are worthy of it.

*If you know your true worth,
you do not need anyone else to confirm it.*

— Alan Cohen

5.

ABOUT THOSE PEOPLE

You know those people. The ones that have made you doubt yourself, the ones that have embarrassed you, talked down to you, talked behind your back, and thrown judgment at you.

When you look at yourself, what do you see? Do you feel proud of the person you see in the mirror?

Try to think back on some comments, opinions, or judgments others have expressed to you that have made you feel inadequate or deflated. We are going to take a minute to focus on each of those people, one at a time, and we are going to use that minute to cut them up. Not in person and not with the intention of being rude! But seriously, think to yourself right now about something you do not like about the way they do things, the choices they make, or their personality. Are they self-absorbed? Cocky? Are they a know-it-all? Do they sit up on their high horse and look down at everyone, including you? Do they portray themselves as perfect with a perfect life and white picket fence? Are they really pretty but vain and superficial? Are they rich? Do they have some sort of power position in a job where they get to feed their ego everyday by acting better than or more powerful than other people? Are they mean? Take what you see on the outside and understand right now what the truth most likely is: that nobody is perfect, nobody's relationship is perfect, and nobody's life is perfect.

THOSE PEOPLE THAT KNOW IT ALL

You know those know-it-alls who think that only they can be right. They are of a very strong-minded personality and they have limited capacity to learn and grow because they already know everything. These people will not develop. They will continue in their world where everything they believe is right with no agreeance to listen to any other perspective or opinion. Their ability to empathize with or understand another person, to walk in another's shoes, is clouded by the self-centred world in which they live in. They are far right, or far left, or far whatever direction, and it is not necessary for you to take anything these people say to heart, nor to let them affect the decisions you make.

You understand that the world is not black and white, that it is very much covered in shades of grey. You know that every person has a story, and your willingness to learn and grow, to hear someone else's perspective, and to put yourself in another person's shoes to empathize with what they may be dealing with makes you a better person.

Pathways in the human brain have conditioned behavioural responses based on experiences a person has had. We all have these conditioned pathways, which is why we fall into habits, get triggered by past events we may not even be consciously aware of, and believe that how we see the world is the "right" way. Some people are more set in believing that only their way of thinking is correct, and they are the know-it-alls of the world. If your self-worth has been affected by a know-it-all, if you have lost confidence in yourself and the decisions you are making because of a know-it-all, label them as such, and let them go. Be proud that you have the capability of learning from the world and the people around you and that you have the character trait that allows you to empathize with others.

When you need to make a decision, sit with it for a while to see if it aligns with your value system and standards you set for yourself. If it feels peaceful in your gut, then it is most likely the right decision for you. We'll dig a little deeper into the decision-making process throughout the book, but for now, smile at those know-it-alls and be humble. Let them continue their seemingly perfect lives in their own little worlds. They have their own lessons to learn.

THOSE PEOPLE THAT ARE JUDGMENTAL

Everyone is guilty of throwing judgment. We all do it. The interesting thing about judgment is that it can be directly related to feelings of envy, resentment, or misaligned values or morals. Think about yourself for a minute and be honest—who in your life have you thrown judgment at? Is it toward the ones that appear perfect in their highlight reels, so skinny, so rich, so in love, so smart? Do you judge those that are well-liked, that seem to make friends everywhere they go, that breeze through their lives buying expensive things and always making it look as though its just so easy to get whatever they want? Do you judge people that have strong opinions or are not afraid of conflict?

Do you judge people based on their career choices? How they parent? How they treat or speak to others?

Two things. One, the highlight reel is a lie. Two, you are judging them because you are either envious of something about them, because you resent them for something, or because you are emotionally triggered by them. This trigger could have been caused by something in your past that you may not be aware of, or it could be from something specific, like how someone has treated you or made you feel.

I want you to think about the people you've thrown judgment at and reflect on which of the causes relates to your feelings. Figure out if it is envy, resentment, or a trigger of your emotions. Once you have narrowed this down, think about the reason behind it. If it is envy, figure out what about this person you are envious of, then begin to form a plan on how to achieve whatever it is in your own life. We'll dig deeper into this when we talk more about comparison. If it is resentment, ask yourself why you feel resentment toward this person. Figure out how this person or their personality relates to your past experiences. Ask yourself what emotions you feel and see what memory comes up to help explain why you feel that way.

All of this being said, it is now time to flip the shoe to the other foot and try to understand why you feel people may be judging you. When people are mean to you, throw judgment at you, or talk behind your back, what we talked about goes both ways: they are envious of something about you, they resent something about you, or something about your personality or actions is triggering something from their past.

As you go through life, you will quickly realize that the more you accomplish, the more you will be judged. Hands down, the times I have been most judged and had the most rude comments made to me was when I was completing my nursing degree while having babies. I have been career-driven ever since I had Ty as a single mom in my twenties, and as my character grew and I learned more about the world, I wanted to advance my career even further for many reasons. Being the abused daughter of an alcoholic gave me more than enough reason to want to become completely independent. I did not ever want to require anything from anyone as I never wanted to have to tolerate being mistreated by anyone, nor allow my children to be dependent on anyone but me.

I knew how much I had to work in order to provide for just myself and Ty, so as my family grew, I knew I would choose the career path that would allow me to make the most money I could while doing the job I had set out to do, all so that I could one day hopefully work less and be there for my children more. I did my nursing degree online so that I could continue to work full time. For the first couple of years, I never told a soul that I was doing it. I wanted to prevent the judgment and opinions of others from causing me to second-guess myself. I knew my confidence wasn't yet strong enough to stand my ground.

Once I had reached the stage where I needed time off work to complete the clinical requirements of my program, I was no longer able to hide my secret career advancement plan. At the time, I was also pregnant with my second baby. From then on, I started to hear judgment almost daily at work. I heard things like, "I can't believe you think you can actually finish it and become an RN," and, "I would never give up my time with my kids to go back to school, I'm not *that* kind of Mom."

My confidence wasn't strong enough to tell them what I would say today. I was terrified of confrontation back then. Years of abuse from my father had taught me to never stand up for myself. So, I accepted those comments. I allowed people to speak rudely to me. I kept my head down and continued to constantly remind myself why I was doing what I was doing. I have a feeling you might relate to this. How I would respond now is conversation in a matter of fact form. It's very simple. I would let them know their comments and opinions on my parenting and career goals are not welcome, and their judgments on how I should run my life are none of my business. Removing emotions from confrontation takes a lot of practise, but once you master it, it eliminates the stress from needed communication.

I completed my nursing degree while on maternity leave with my third baby. When I returned to work, the comments and judgment worsened. Most of it came from a couple of my once-fellow LPNs that had either tried and quit pursuing their nursing degrees, or had otherwise made the decision not to advance their careers for whatever reason. Some of it also came from my RNs that I had once worked under but had now become "equal" to. A few of these RNs offered their congrats and support, many said nothing, but a few were mean. The mean ones passive aggressively challenged many of the decisions I made as their team lead and eventual charge nurse. I went through many days of taking deep breaths and accepting the comments and rudeness from these people. My current self would have handled these people a lot differently, I can assure you. Today, I would smile in response to these comments. I would politely inform them that I spent many hours and much effort completing my Bachelor of Science in Nursing degree, and the education, experience and knowledge I hold allows me to confidently and competently perform my job as Charge Nurse. The job upper management has placed me to do. I would invite them to contribute any ideas they have towards the situation at hand only if it had direct relation to the patients they were attending to, and to refrain from offering any personal judgements on how I make decisions as team lead. Giving yourself credit for your accomplishments and disallowing inappropriate judgments will help you respond to others with assurance and create invisible boundaries that tell the other person it will not be tolerated. You have to stop the bully.

I have worked hard to become more assertive and to gain enough confidence to stand strong in how I expect to be treated and how I expect others to be treated. I do believe it is in my soul to be overly kind and accepting of people—I get that from my mother. She stood by and endured my father's abuse all her life, so I have worked to find a balance between being a passive pushover and not losing my kindness. Isn't that a hard balance? Back to nature versus nurture again!

OUTSIDE OF NORMAL

It's so easy to say, "Overcome your fear and change your life," but in all honesty, people around us make it very hard to do that sometimes. I really hate how people think you are weird if you do things outside of the "normal" way. I'm so sick of it. Get married young, have babies, have a healthy and successful marriage, get a big new house, build a career, put your kids in every sport at the most competitive level because they are better than the other kids, talk mostly about your kids because they are your whole world, don't let anyone know if anyone in your family makes a wrong choice that takes away from the perfection of the white picket fence you have built around your house and the family inside of it.

My favourite judgmental statement right now is, "You're pregnant? But you have a nineteen-year-old and you are thirty-nine. Four kids with a spread that far apart? You must be crazy."

I was sitting in a local coffee shop writing this book, and a girl I went to high school with walked in.

"Hey Dena! How's it going?"

We started catching up a bit, and that of course meant talking about what the kids were all doing. As she scurried off to her son's hockey game, she scoffed and said, "Oh, and good luck with the baby apparently," while her judgment-filled eyes made contact with my baby belly.

"Thanks!" I excitedly replied. So, two things here. One, she already knew I was expecting so a congratulations would have been a lot more appropriate than the scoff she gave me, and two, she could go right ahead and hurry off to her life with all the perfection she was always boasting about.

This girl I went to school with was one of the ones that don't stray from the normal. She had a typical, perfectly timed family, got married young, had three babies, put them all in the most prestigious camps and academies, spent every night running to all of their numerous events, and talked and posted constantly about it all. Every game win, every trophy, every perfect moment. The highlight reel, and an ignorant comment for anyone not doing the same.

Well, I said it earlier: I don't live my life in the "normal" way. I had a seriously different childhood that significantly changed the way I look at life. So, I live mine however I want and however it makes me happy. And with that comes judgment. I want a big family because for the first time in my life, I am surrounded by people that love me unconditionally and I love them all to the depths of my soul. It makes my heart full to love them all as much as I do and to care for and nurture them in ways that fill my soul, and it makes me feel complete to have them love me back just for being their loving mom. I have also had numerous experiences while meditating where I've seen visions of my life before it happens, and this baby has been in my meditations and visions for four years now. I have a strong intuition has never led me astray up to this point in my life, so I have learned to trust in it. Every time I didn't listen to it, I regretted it, as my choices against it led me down paths I shouldn't have gone down.

I had the privilege of being a young mom in my early twenties, and now I have the privilege of being a mom in my wiser years. I am thankful for both in so many ways. When I told my grandpa I was having another baby he replied, "That's terrible news! Why in the hell would you go and do that?" He told me I was too old to be having a baby and that I had enough kids. Wow grandpa, warm my heart why don't you.

I love how people talk sometimes, with no regard for basic manners and definitely no barrier in telling you their strong-ass opinions. Should I allow him to hurt my feelings? Probably not. But he was so good to me in the past, and he's my grandpa, so I let it go. Plus, I had tried standing up to him once before and it didn't go well. He started saying rude things a lot more frequently after that and I don't have it in me to battle him. He's getting older, lost my grandma, and isn't enjoying this stage of his life as much as maybe the thought he might. Does that make it OK to treat me like he does sometimes? No, it doesn't, but sometimes you have to pick your battles based on how much you feel like battling and how guilty you might feel if you say something you might regret. Is it OK for the old high school friend to stroll on over to my table at the coffee shop and drop a scoff and a condescending wish of good luck? No, but again, I pick my battles. I don't care enough about our old friendship to ever rekindle it, so she can think whatever she wants. I know what I want in my life.

The point of all of this is that I will die on the mountain of protesting judgment from other people who try to make you feel like shit for living your life how you want to live it. It makes me really mad, because for every choice I have made to better my life, I have gotten push-back and digs. I have learned to rise above it, remember the bigger picture in life, and make the changes anyway—but it is these kinds of remarks from people that can hinder you from wanting to change. I am here to strongly remind you that all of those people you are going to run into can take a hike. That's not the phrase I say in my head... but much more appropriate for your reading pleasure.

People can sure change you. They can challenge you or hurt you with their judgments, and this can cause you to start to become someone you were not meant to become. As this happens, it can feel like you are losing yourself, like you don't know who you are or who you should be anymore. It can get so confusing. For those of you currently in this process, I'm guessing that's why you were pulled to this book. Most of you are likely of a people-pleasing nature: passive, but trying to build up the self-worth and confidence that experiences and other people have somehow destroyed in you. You weren't born thinking that you're not enough. So, keep reading, and we'll work on finding that trust and love in yourself again. It's in there, I promise.

THOSE PEOPLE THAT ARE MEAN

Some people really do become products of their environments. If you sit down with anyone that has been mean to someone, you will learn that at some point in their life, someone else was mean to them. Their response to being hurt is causing hurt. Humans have a natural, animalistic quality that makes them want to retaliate when hurt or angered. Only a few of us respond to hurt with a more submissive demeanour and with an understanding that we would never want to make someone else feel how we were made to feel. With the percentage of abusers that have been abused, I am astonished at how so few of us exist out there that refuse to continue the cycle. I am writing a whole separate book on this topic because I believe that this is where most worldly problems lie: in the cycle of abuse and in actions caused by pain.

When children grow up in abusive environments, it becomes all they know. Abuse becomes a normal way of treating people. Well, this is a mountain I will die on, shouting out to the world: violence and abuse of any form is not normal. It is not how we were created to treat each other. When we replace hurtful actions with loving ones, the pieces of our souls slowly get put back together. Children and others who have endured abuse deserve to know that there is a better life out there for them.

I began to learn about mean people when I was little, but at the time, I didn't know they were mean. To me, they were normal. It is only now that I can look back at my life and see the meanness in people. If I could have one wish in the world, it would be that those hurt by others could realize that their behaviour is not acceptable. Well, actually if I could have one wish, it would really just be for people to stop hurting other people. That sounds like a better wish.

For those of you that have been dealing with any form of abuse, physical, verbal, or manipulative, from anyone in your life, you must understand that the abuse is not about you. You must understand that those that hurt others have pain inside themselves that they either refuse to deal with or do not know how to deal with.

It is hardest to understand meanness when the people being mean are those closest to you, and this meanness is also the hardest to let go of. I don't remember much about my life prior to the age of five, but my mother tells me that I annoyed my father from the beginning. When I was a baby, she would hide me from him if I cried so that he couldn't hurt me. He carried anger toward my mother and me all throughout my childhood, and when he drank it got worse. Looking back at myself as a young child turned teenage girl, it was no wonder I had no self-worth into my adulthood.

I still wonder why my father showed such anger toward me right from the beginning, but after finding out a little of his story and working on my own healing, I now understand that it has nothing to do with the value of my being. In the same way, other people's actions do not have anything to do with the value of your being. This is a lesson I must keep reminding myself of though, as once we have an ideology in our heads, it is hard to reprogram. Don't be too hard on yourself during this learning curve. It's not a quick process.

The meanness in people does not define us. We cannot let it. You will not lose yourself to them. You are a product of your decisions, not of your circumstances. The only thing you can control is your reactions and what you choose to do with the hurt from your past. You can use it to become stronger, or you can let it debilitate you.

When I started working in the emergency room, it was like God handing me this ongoing abuse problem on a silver platter. So many people suffering with their mental health, all of whom had stories of abuse. Each and every one of them. And not one of them had any self-worth or self-love. When I looked in their eyes, they were empty. Their souls had been so dimmed that they were just like empty physical bodies walking around with no purpose in their lives, no idea why they mattered, and no indication of just how special they were. These were people of every age, young to old. I asked every single one of them what their story was, and every single one of them was a product of maltreatment and pain.

ABOUT THOSE PEOPLE

For most of these patients, we had to use bed restraints. Under the Mental Health Act, we had to keep them hospitalized for twenty-four hours to allow time for assessment and to keep them and others free from harm. From there, they would either be admitted for further assessment and treatment or let back into the destructive world that was all they knew.

I decided I couldn't continue to just be part of the Band-Aid team. Not when I knew what I knew. Not when I knew just how damn hard it was to endure pain, and how amazing it was to come out on the other side of it. To feel love and respect for oneself, confidence, a full heart, gratitude, joy, and to be surrounded by love. It was and is something worth fighting for.

Now that we've talked about the reason why people are mean, it's time to ask the question: what do you do about people that are mean to you? It's such a simple answer, but it will require an action not as simple to complete. What you must do is remove yourself from the hurtful situation and remove the hurtful person from your life if they are not willing to stop mistreating you. That's it. We'll touch more on healing from hurt and letting go through forgiveness, but these are the first, most important steps.

You may find yourself having trouble recognizing a pattern of abuse (manipulative abuse is the hardest to detect). When I got confused trying to figure out what behaviour toward me was acceptable, I was told by my dear friend and nursing instructor to think of my daughter. They asked me, "How would you feel if your daughter was being treated by her father, brother, friend, or boyfriend in the same way that you are?"

Oh! What a light bulb went off in my head. The exercise was so simple, but it showed me that I wasn't thinking of myself with respect and with self-worth in the same way that I think of my beautiful daughter, Esmee. "Well, I wouldn't be OK with it!" I replied.

It all became so clear, so quickly, even after years of not understanding or being able to recognize how I deserve to be treated. Again, abuse was all I had ever known since I was little, and so to deserve it was an expectation my father had set for me. It can all seem so complicated. It can make you question if you were being too sensitive around behaviours towards you and it can leave you feeling very confused as to why your defence mechanisms are constantly warning you that the way they are speaking to you, and handling situations is not right. Your warning flags do not ring off with people unless there is a reason. With most people, you just interact without having to think about it, or reflect on the interaction.

Narcissism is a personality disorder in which the person is acting with a sense of self-importance, a preoccupation of power and entitlement, a lack of empathy, and arrogance. It is commonly displayed in behaviour's such as avoidance to personal trauma or internalized pain, and those expressing these tendencies become manipulative to others in attempt to hold control or gain power over others. If you have ever experienced this with a loved one, it is extremely confusing as it causes you to constantly second guess your actions or words as being the sole cause to the troubled relationship. It's funny how our emotional attachments to people can cloud our ability to see unacceptable behaviour. Manipulative abuse is the toughest to spot because abusers make you think that you're being paranoid and that you're creating the behaviours as an illusion in your mind. It's feels like a game they are playing with you. It's not a fun game. The term is gaslighting, and it's used to describe irrational behaviours often displayed by a manipulator or someone with narcissistic personality disorder. These behaviours include refusal to admit when they are wrong, and attempts to convince the other person he or she is paranoid about an improper action they are confronting the accuser about.

Through all of the work I did on healing, trauma, boundaries and learning how to deal with other people, I was able to finally find my voice. Trust is a hard thing to gain back once it's lost, and once the character of a person changes, it is hard to believe that a breach of trust will never happen again. It may not be necessary to end your relationship with a person who is hurting you or causing unnecessary toxicity in your life if, and only if, the person is willing to change the offensive behaviour, and two, to show you that by speaking your truth and being honest about your feelings, you can release the toxicity within your body that would eventually have caused you harm, leaving you feeling relieved and free from the burden of the pain you had buried deep inside you. This is very important because it is this type of buried pain that creates anxiety, anger, and sadness, and which can eventually affect your physical health. We'll talk more about the link between emotional pain and physical health in part two.

To use as a guide for when to remove yourself from others' toxicity, here is an analogy a counselor working with Alberta Alcohol and Drug Abuse Comission once told me when I was seeking professional help for my family of alcoholics: A person working through addiction or other great challenges requiring change is climbing a mountain. They may stumble and fall a bit, but if they only fall a short distance and are able to find their footing, get back up, and continue the climb, then you are safe to continue to offer your support to them. If they fall right off the mountain, then you must remove yourself from supporting them because only they can decide whether to stay at the bottom or climb back up. Not enabling unacceptable behaviour is a boundary everyone must learn, and that work is internal—only you can change the way you allow people to treat you. If they are not willing to climb, you must let them go until they are. Enabling them only worsens their problem and allows them to continue living in the same toxic environment, no matter who gets hurt. Letting a loved one go is one of the hardest things you will ever have to do in your life. But this guideline is one that I now live by.

Relationships are about give and take, so each person must be willing to change the things that are affecting the other in a negative way. If a person is not willing to change, or has shown continued toxic behaviour, then you, having set your boundary, should remove them from your life. For some of you, doing so may put you in a dangerous situation, so be sure to use your resources, like your local police and medical professionals via abuse hotlines or the emergency room. They can put you in contact with social workers and psychiatric medical staff for assistance. For those of you dealing with a higher level of abuse, I am writing a book that focuses on guiding you toward breaking the cycle and supporting you in dealing with the pain and traumatic emotions involved.

We'll talk more about setting healthy boundaries later in part two, but you should know that boundaries are the secret to self-respect. Setting boundaries helps you create a road map for detecting toxicity in the people you have in your life. For now, just consider how you recognize toxic people in your life. I focus on how I feel when I am with them. When you are with a friend or family member that makes you feel peaceful and recharged, understands you, makes you smile, and legitimately feeds your soul, you know they are good for you. When you are with someone that causes you to feel a yellow or red defence flag go up in your chest or stomach, one that makes you feel uncomfortable in being yourself and leaves you feeling irritated, angry, or sad, they are not good for your soul.

THOSE PEOPLE THAT ARE PASSIVE AGGRESSIVE

What about that person that makes comments about you or your life, leaving you feeling not very good about yourself after hanging out with them? These people are mean in a certain way. They're passive aggressive, and most of their actions and words come out of envy, resentment, or as projections of their own unhappiness. It is about something you have that they wish they had. Maybe it's the house you live in, your body shape, or your wardrobe. Maybe it's the amount of money you have or the baby you have when they have been having trouble conceiving. Maybe your child has qualities they wish their child possessed, or maybe you're the kind of parent they wish they were. Or maybe it's about your career, the relationships you hold, or the way you always seem so calm and put together.

Many times, I've come home feeling down after talking with a work colleague, a random nurse I came into contact with on shift, an old acquaintance, or another mom. Afterward, I would ask myself, why does my gut feel like that person wasn't being very nice to me? Have you ever experienced this? Where someone makes a comment to you that your gut instantly doesn't like, but you second-guess yourself and think, *Maybe I'm reading too much into it*, or, *Maybe it's all in my head*.

I'm going to tell you right now, it is absolutely not all in your head. You listen to that gut because it is telling you the honest truth.

You see, our gut feeling is our intuition, our inner guidance, and it holds the wisdom of the soul. The soul is who we really are, and it is far more advanced than the ego. Know that the ego is a separate entity from the soul, and it is through the ego that we are made to feel inferior to another person. Once you are completely confident in the person you are, you get control of your ego and you are able to let things go a lot more easily. To be able to let go of people's comments, knowing full well that they are not about you but rather about their own internal problems, releases you from bitterness and anger. It can still hurt, but it won't stay with you once you are able to identify this truth.

The one thing about passive aggressive people is that they will never admit feelings of envy or resentment to you because it would make them feel inferior. They may not even realize that they are envious, but they do feel that being mean to you makes them feel better about themselves, which is why they continue to do it, oblivious to how it makes you feel. This goes for the stay-at-home mamas versus the working mamas, the skinnier girl versus the heavier set girl, the extremely intelligent person versus the average smart person—you get the point.

Removing mean and passive aggressive people or people that affect you in a negative way is soul cleansing. It will be one of the hardest things you must get used to doing, however once you have done it a couple times, the steps get easier and you begin to really feel the effects of removing toxicity from your life.

THOSE PEOPLE THAT ARE SELF-CENTRED

You know that friend or family member. The one that you have to put all of the effort into maintaining a relationship with. They are in their own self-centred world and if you stopped calling or texting, the relationship would fall off. Which friend or family member are you picturing right now?

Did you know that you don't deserve to be in any kind of relationship where the other person doesn't care how you are or care to be there to support you when you need it the most? Your standards for friendships and personal relationships are about to change. No longer will you allow yourself to spend your time on anyone that doesn't care to spend their time with you. That's it. You simply do not deserve it.

Love these people where they are at and let them go. Forgive them for becoming so self-absorbed, understand that it may not be about you, and even if it is about you, if they have left it unaddressed, then it is no longer your problem. You shouldn't have to guess what you may or may not have said or done wrong. If they choose to let go of you rather than opening up communication to save your relationship, then they are not worth your love, energy, or time. Get them out of your life. Today.

A LESSON TO BE LEARNED

Here's the most amazing thing about understanding people and their poor behaviour: they are just living in their own little worlds, dealing with their own struggles and life challenges, and they do not know how to properly address or even recognize their emotions or their related actions. The funny thing about all of these people is that they were my life lessons the whole time: your greatest teachers in life are your biggest challenges. So, take whoever is causing you your greatest challenge and figure out what you are meant to learn from them. This is the best secret to dealing with people and should be a method you add to your survival kit in order to substantially decrease the stress, sadness, anger, and frustration that come with your inability to control other people's actions.

My learning lesson this whole time was to stop letting people treat me poorly. That's it! All of those people that kept coming into my life, making me feel bad about myself and making me feel defeated because I couldn't find the words to speak up for my own self-worth were all there to help me find my voice. To help me to start standing up for the little girl inside of me, that scared and vulnerable little girl that so badly needed me to stand up for her, to protect her, and to make her feel safe and loved.

These life lessons always have to do with you. You need to ask yourself what you are doing to attract these people or these situations into your life. You need to ask yourself, what is my learning lesson here? Psychologist Gay Hendricks describes the rule of three, where if the same thing happens to you three times or more, then it's because of you, and not anybody else.

Becoming aware of why you feel the way you do and why these challenges and limits show up for you can be very helpful. It will make it so that it no longer takes a catastrophic event for you to finally learn a lesson. It does require a high level of emotional intelligence to have the ability to recognize when you're in the midst of a learning lesson though. In most cases, your reaction to hurt and your emotions around that pain cloud the lesson. The tricky thing is, is when you are in the middle of learning lessons, you have not yet developed a higher emotional intelligence—this usually comes from the after-effects of such lessons.

If you can hear my words and understand the concept here, listen to me when I say figure out that learning lesson. It will save you from having to endure repeated challenges that continue to show up until you do get it. I never had the courage, strength, or know-how to fight my own battles and stand up for the little girl inside of me until much later in life. But nobody can fight our battles for us. It's up to us. That's the whole point. The power of independence is learning to fight your own battles so that you can always find a way to feel safe. You can always get what your soul needs, and you can obtain peace and contentment in your body. Now practicing the art and internal work of change after that light bulb goes off? Not easy. But walk through it. You'll come out a fucking butterfly after all of it. Shed that caterpillar skin and fly. It's going to feel amazing.

"Not everything that is faced can be changed, but nothing can be changed until it is faced."
— James Baldwin

6.

TIME TO BE HONEST

This question is important, so actually answer it: Are you happy? Truly?

Don't give the kind of fluff answer that we all say day-to-day.
"Hi, how are you?"
"I'm good, thanks. And you?"
"I'm good."

What a polite world we live in to constantly ask this question. The worst is at drive-through windows. You pull up to the window speaker and the person says, "Hi there, how are you doing today?" Seriously? Am I supposed to answer this truly? What shall I say? "I'm doing terrible, I have a lot of things going on in my life. How are you?" What would the drive-through person say? Maybe it would be silently awkward for a minute, and then they would say, "Sorry to hear that." Maybe they would buy you your latte to help brighten your day? Either way, do people actually want to hear the real answer when we ask this question?

Polite habits are fine and all, but it's time to actually think about your answer to the question, how are you doing? Now I don't know about you, but I'm not going to start telling the Starbucks employee my life story, but there is something to be said about actually asking ourselves that question. How am I? It's so basic, but we all live in busy worlds and we can forget to take the time to check in with ourselves. You would check in on a friend, so why not on yourself?

Ask yourself, *How am I doing?* Follow it up with, *In what areas of my life do I feel most happy?* and, *In what areas of my life am I not happy?*

HOW DO WE KNOW WE NEED TO CHANGE THINGS?

In our everyday lives, we wake up each day and feel a certain way. When we are happy, we wake up in light mood, excited, energetic, and interested in people and in the work we do. We laugh, smile, care about things big and small, and have a desire to help people or help change things to make the world a better place. When we are happy in our place of work, our soul feels energized after our day.

When we are unhappy, we wake up tired, uninterested, stressed, irritable, overwhelmed, tense, and angry. Our care for the world and the people in it is low. When we are unhappy in our place of work, our soul feels drained at the end of the day. Burnout feels constant. Finding energy feels impossible, no matter how much we rest.

Happy versus unhappy is basic stuff, but to be quite honest, I am finding that people are so used to being unhappy that they don't actually recognize that they are anymore—it has just become their normal way of living.

For those that have experienced happiness before, think back to this time and try to remember what each emotion you had felt like. Think back to past desires and passion that surrounded them

For those that have had a very hard story and have never had the opportunity to truly feel happiness, think way back, perhaps to a time in your childhood, when, for even just a moment in time, you felt some happiness.

What everyone must know and must regularly be reminded of is that living on autopilot has become normal in this world. We just accept each day as it is, stay in the same situations for too long, and put up with the same crap we shouldn't be accepting from people. This becomes our normal. We are too busy to take the time to slow down and recognize our emotions, process them, and relate them to past experiences. We worry too far into the future to focus on the present. I know, I know, it sounds so simple. *But that's the problem*—we have forgotten the basics. We have become lost in our own worlds, spending too much time comparing and becoming overwhelmed with the fear of failure, the fear of being judged, and the fear of change.

What we must know and be able to recognize is that once we determine that there is an area or many areas in our lives that are causing unhappy feelings, that it is our cue that we need to change something. We must overcome the fear of change, figure out what it is our soul is trying to direct us to, and then find a way to accomplish it.

> *"Have more than you show,*
> *and speak less than you know."*
> — William Shakespeare

7.

THE JONESES ARE ASSHOLES

Keeping up with the amazing Joneses. The rat race. The pretend amazing life and perfectly painted white picket fence. All of it to help us all feel like we are not doing anything well enough. Fear of change may be very common, but when you look around, it seems everyone else is doing things with ease. Social media is a blessing in so many ways, however it is absolutely a major cause of depression, anxiety, and comparison without realistic thought. Everyone has a highlight reel, but if you actually talk to the person or examine the life inside that reel, you will find that it is very misleading.

Everyone seems to be doing things bigger and better and living lives that are so much more than yours, and you have no idea how they do it. How do they afford all the things they have? How is she so skinny? Why does their marriage seem so perfect when mine doesn't always feel that way... or ever? How do they have the time to be doing all these fun things when most of my time is spent working and running around? How does that mom seem so relaxed and content all the time?

This is *comparison without facts*. It's such a dangerous way of living. Depression is souring around this world, and people have forgotten how to be grateful for the things they have. This is a direct result of comparison without facts. We must remember that people lie. They do not always tell the truth! In particular, the people with the lowest self-esteem and self-worth pretend, lie, and make things seem not as they truly are. They will look you in the face and lie as if they either truly believe themselves or they need to make sure you never find out what is actually going on in their lives. Well, in a world full of depression and feelings of inadequacy, I'm so tired of people making other people feel like shit. It's time to be honest with each other so that we no longer feel alone in the life happenings that may fall in front of us, especially the ones we can't control.

The ones that lie are the ones that most need to read this book. Their self-worth, self-esteem, and confidence are so incredibly low that they feel they must pretend and put on a show to make it seem like none of the bad stuff is happening to them. If you have ever pretended before, or if you still do, it's time to do yourself a favour and get real. You cannot live your life pretending. The house of cards you are trying to build will absolutely crumble. You must be honest in your life experiences to be able to look problems in the face and actually fix them. Living a lie just doesn't work. And the world doesn't need to hear your mistruths.

Do yourself a favour and find authentic people that you can use as a sounding board, or study how they do certain things. Comparison *with* facts is what can provide opportunity for ideas for change. Start studying the lifestyles of people you admire, and you'll start to acquire more information about what possibilities are out there for you and what kind of lifestyle you want to be living.

Now, for those of you that still compare yourselves to others—which is all of us—read on.

ENVY IS A KEY

Feeling envious, showing unhappiness over someone else's good fortune, desiring to have the same. Oh, envy. Always thought of as a negative emotion. I used to hate feeling envious of people over the things they had, the relationships they had, the way they looked, the careers they had, the money they made, the kids they had, the blessings they had been given. What I didn't understand is that envy does not have to be a negative emotion. *It is a key to what you actually want.* Here are questions you can ask yourself in order to start using this emotion to get what you want, rather than allowing it to create resentment, anger, or disappointment toward the person you are envious of.

1. *Who are you envious of?*
2. *What do they possess* that you feel envious of?
   - A. *Is it a character trait?* Are they always so energetic and happy? Do they attract people everywhere they go? Is their body shape something you wish yours looked like? Do they parent their child the way you wish you could? Do they seem so patient all the time? Look at the character trait that you are

most envious of and understand that it is something you wish was part of your character. If you wanted to be kind and patient at heart, you would never be envious of someone that was mean to people or short-tempered. If you wanted to be more fit and have more muscle tone and less fat on your body, you would never be envious of someone who was overweight and carried much fat on their body. Think about the character trait you are envious of, and rather than resent the person for having it, use your envy to acquire the trait for yourself.

B. *Is it their relationships?* Do you see a happy marriage? Do you love the relationship they have with their children, parents, siblings, friends? What part of their relationships are you the most envious of? Do they seem more romantic in their love life? Is it the respect they have for their partner? Do they communicate well? You would never be envious of someone that fights all the time in their relationships, or someone who is talked down to, manipulated, or abused in their relationships. Figure out what part of this person's relationships you feel envious of and study it. This is how you figure out what you desire in your relationships, and what might be missing.

C. *Is it their career?* Is it about how much money they make? Is it about status? Do you wish you were more fulfilled in your career? Is it the type of work they are doing? Are you a stay-at-home mom that feels envious of how a working mom has something outside of her role at home? Are you a working mom that feels envious of how a stay-at-home mom has more time to spend with her family? Again, these are all signs for what you really want in your life. You would never be envious of someone whose career is something you would never want to do, so figure out what you are envious of, then figure out what you need to do to acquire it.

D. *Is it their lifestyle?* Do they travel a lot? Do they live somewhere you feel envious of? What is it about that location you are envious of? Is it a quieter place, is there water, is the scenery beautiful? Is it busier with more people and opportunity? Do they move a lot and see different parts of the world? Do they have roots and a community you desire? Figure it out.

Comparison and the rat race are real things, especially when you enter your thirties. Once you start looking around at others, it is so important to keep what you want out of your story, what your values are, and what you want to fulfill you in check. You must remember that everyone has a different story, different life experiences, and different support systems in place. No life is like another. Focus on how to create and improve yours.

So, we talked about how to recognize the need for change based on envy, and you have figured out what area or areas of your life you want to change. What do you think comes next?

The hard part...

"Change will not come if we wait for some other person or some other time. We are the ones we've been waiting for. We are the change that we seek."
— Barack Obama

8.

HOW TO CHANGE THINGS

If there is one thing that never changes in this world, it is that everything changes. Everyone has a story. No matter how good yours is, or how bad it is, it is up to you to change how things are. You are the writer in the story of your life, so you have to be the one to change the story. Happiness is solely up to you. Once you realize this, you have to develop trust in yourself that you can change things. Once you develop this trust, you develop a power that is stronger than anyone can imagine and that no one can ever take away. If you have ever experienced pain in your life, change is where you use the pain to find the courage you need to change your life. Change is how you respond to the people and happenings in your life.

We are products of our environments, but we don't have to be just that. Nature and nurture is a brilliant combination, but if we don't start living our lives with proper perspective, we end up lost in the nurture that moulds us. The proximity principle is a direct example of this environmental influence. It states that we mould to become like the ten people closest to us. The country in which we live, the culture around us, the people with whom we are surrounded, the values and belief systems that we are taught—this is our nurture. Our nature is the innate compass we hold deep in our souls; the inner workings of what makes us who we are. Finding a way to honour and trust in the love and capable hands of our creator is the direct path to inner peace and strength. Once we can reflect on the events of the past and use them to better understand ourselves, then we can plunge forward into becoming the person we were created to be.

LIVING ON AUTOPILOT

One thing I've come to be very aware of in my thirties is the difference between living on autopilot and living in focus. I spent many of my earlier years going through the motions: wake up, shower, get my son ready, kiss him goodbye as I guiltily drop him off at daycare, go to work, have the same thoughts repeatedly enter my mind, have the same emotions triggered from the repetitive thoughts, converse with co-workers, finish work, pick up my son, hug him and kiss him, play outside, make us some dinner, get ready for bed. I visited routinely with the same friends and continued to wonder each day, *What am I meant to be doing?*

I'll tell you: you're meant to be figuring out what you want, one step at a time, and listening to the signs of your strengths.

When my younger brother died, I was eighteen years old. In the few days we spent with him in the pediatric ICU, when I lay my head to rest each sleep shift, I thought about many things. I thought about all the times I shared with him growing up, I thought about how he must be feeling as he lay unconscious in his coma, I thought about how much I already missed him, and I thought about the nurses. Some were so kind and compassionate, and they made the toughest moments somehow bearable. Some were quiet and sharp, but when the alarms went off on his machines, they knew their job so well that they kept bringing him back to us.

The next time I was in the ICU was with my mom. Again, I watched the nurses focus as they worked to continue to keep her alive.

I spent eight years in my twenties living on autopilot, working at a restaurant, day in, day out. My focus was on keeping my son happy, healthy, and fed. But something was missing inside me. One day, one of my best guy friends stopped in to visit me at work. He told me, "Go to school and become a nurse." It was like a light turned on in my brain. I thought about it for a while. I weighed out my options. I applied. I got in. I was terrified, but *that was it*. I had not been paying attention to the earlier signs, to my constant thoughts of the nurses during my family's struggles. I hadn't even thought about it until my friend stopped in and told me to go to nursing school. God sent him that day because I just wasn't getting it on my own.

PAYING ATTENTION TO GUIDANCE

During any process of change and self-growth, you will attract people that will offer to help you on your path. I believe that's God directly placing people in front of you. If you pray for answers, start paying attention to who comes into your life and what they have to say. If you pray for support, guidance, and knowledge, see who you meet. It is one of the coolest things to look back after and be able to clearly see how the puzzle pieces fell together.

Looking back, there were so many times in my life when I needed something, and someone just appeared. One specific time I remember so clearly was when I was in my early twenties. I had been dealing with a whole lot of problems from the toxicity caused by my alcoholic parents. I was searching for God again at this time, as the last time I had felt his presence was when I had been eighteen years old and my younger brother had passed away. I wanted to feel the presence of the spirit world again so that I wouldn't feel so lost, defeated in earthly problems bigger than me, and alone.

I had just gotten off night shift at the hospital and was dropping my son off at his school when another mom came by. She was polite and kind, and after she introduced herself, we exchanged a bit of small talk.

I was so tired from working all night that it was all I could do to see Ty head in safely through the school doors en route to class before I was off to bed. As I lay down, that mom's face passed through my thoughts. Something about her eyes had grabbed my attention. But then off I fell to sleep.

When I woke up to pick Ty up from school, she was there again. She came over to me and started another conversation. This time, she brought up God and mentioned that her husband was a Lutheran preacher at a church in town. Then she invited me for coffee. Something inside of me just made me say yes. We ended up talking for a couple hours while our boys played, and that one coffee date turned into three or four more as the weeks went by that month. She taught me some scriptures and gave me my first ever bible as a gift. I was introduced to God again. I'll never forget her.

Shortly after, I started hanging out more with a friend I had met through work. We had great talks every time we got together, with wine and laughter. We talked about everything in life: relationships, past hurts, parties, kids, being moms, being wives, being single, family, childhood. One weekend night, we had a sleepover. After the kids went to bed, we had a couple glasses of wine, and somehow, she began telling me this crazy story about a time when she was on a trip with her friend, sleeping, and a devil spirit had entered her room. She described every detail like it had happened yesterday; she was still terrified. This being had stood over her as she lay in bed, a black cloud with a deep, growling voice, and she had felt her throat start to close—the evil spirit was choking her. When she had tried to scream, only a muffled sound came out, as if someone had gagged her. She had looked over at her friend in the other bed who could see everything happening. The friend had immediately started to pray. She had prayed to God to remove the evil spirit from her friend and to cover them with a blanket of protection. Suddenly, the spirit had diminished to a small grey cloud with what sounded like a muffled roar before completely vanishing into thin air. Both of the girls had stared at each other in complete disbelief.

My friend cried as she relived the story. She told me she had not told anyone about it, as people would think she was crazy. After her experience, she and her friend had started studying the bible profusely. They prayed every day and started attending church to enhance their faith and continue to grow their blanket of protection to reach across their families so that they were never bothered again.

In her studies, she learned of spirits being sent from heaven to earth and that some of them are healers, some are teachers, and some are warriors sent to help fight off evil on earth. She told me that she was sent as a warrior, and so evil attacked her directly. After her experience, she had a deep longing to learn as much as she could about the battle between good and evil and to pass her teachings on to others.

One thing I always found in my beautiful friend with gorgeous dark features and deep brown eyes was that she was a fighter. She was assertive and strong. She held strong beliefs and had an untouchable value system. Her mother was the same. Strong, strong women of the world. They were like protectors of the weak, with hearts as kind as could be. There was a grace about these two women that I felt mesmerized by when I first met them. My friend really was amazing. Her husband was a police officer, and he was also the nicest, sweetest guy you could ever meet. They had three beautiful children that they were raising to be kind, sweet, and strong—my favourite combo.

My beautiful friend taught me that I was sent from heaven to earth as a healer. It was then that I realized why I had been pushed toward nursing from numerous nudges. I also realized that I needed to find a way to heal my hurt so that I could continue to help others, as it was my soul's purpose to do. God sent my friend to me the day we met. That's two.

The third life teacher God sent me in that short period of time was my nursing instructor. During my time at nursing school, we slowly developed a relationship, and as it grew, we began to talk about the deepest, darkest secrets each of us held about our pasts. Not many people knew my story, and when I started to talk to her, I found I wasn't alone in the awful things that had happened to me. As she told her story, I was in awe of the pain she had endured, and how strong she was when she talked about it. She told me that I had sounded strong too, but I sure didn't feel it inside.

Thirteen years later, our relationship is as strong as ever, filled with three-hour-long coffee dates every few months. She is hands down a saviour to me, with her life skills and knowledge, helping me to understand people and how they work, why they do the things they do, and how to empathize with them even through the toughest of times. She works with Victim Services now as a side job after I told her how she absolutely saved me during my darkest challenges just by listening, understanding my feelings, and helping me understand and deal with the actions of a wrong-doer in my life. She had no idea that she had been that helpful—that is how humble she is.

Now that I have grown into the person I am today, our talks are a lot lighter on traumatic events, but we still dive deep into relationships, people, jobs, kids, and life moments every time I see her. She became my mentor as I learned how to become a healer on a deeper level than just nursing the physical health of people. God sent her to me, and I remember the first time I met her just as clearly as I do the other two beautiful people he sent me. It's like something in you just knows to stop for a minute and pay attention to these people. It's something about their eyes and the look in them when you first make eye contact with them.

I have so many more experiences with people being dropped into my life like this, but I'll talk more about them as I go through how to find your path throughout the rest of this book. There we will talk about how to spot these kinds of experiences that can help you acknowledge the path you are being directed to walk down. Your soul will thank you. For now, I want you to see how relationships are such a huge part of your battle gear. So, stop trying so hard to seek who it is you think you need. Who you think you need is who your ego wants and who it seems impossible to find.

Speaking of impossible to find, the same principles apply in the dating world too. This is for all of you out there that are trying to find "the one." Dating is so hard. One of the most important things you need to know is that when finding "the one" seems hard, it is because your ego is taking over. Stop trying to micromanage what your head thinks it wants and allow your soul to start talking. You will start to hear an inner narrative when you release control. Who you actually need will be placed right in front of you, so keep listening, follow your gut feelings, and watch it unfold. Pray for what you seek, and watch yourself attract everything you have ever wanted. Think of yourself as the middle piece of a puzzle, and once you're settled into place, the other pieces just fall around you to complete the whole picture.

I absolutely love stories about people. I can't wait to hear yours.

PLANNING FOR CHANGE

If someone told you to close your eyes and picture your dream self, who would you be? What titles would you have? What would you look like? How old would you be? What would your demeanour be? Write this all down.

Go into nature, into grass or snow, and find quiet. Start taking deep breaths and listen to whatever it is that comes to your mind first. When do you feel the best? What are your hobbies? What makes your soul excited when you think about doing it? Write these down.

If you can't think of answers on your own, ask the people closest to you, like friends, family, or co-workers. Write all their answers down.

If you still don't know the answers to some of these questions, try joining a class of some sort. Here you can make new connections with people, learn what you like or do not like, and start recognizing when passion and excitement fills up inside of you.

Now, think back to your life story. Is there a pattern or repetitive connection attached to anything you wrote down? Have you had a nagging nudge that you may not have been paying attention to? Think about the hints, and write them all down. Then, write down all your strengths. Be honest here—this is not the time to be modest.

Once you have chosen what it is you really want, it's time to take action. When you do, be sure to listen to your gut. Your gut is God. It is your ethical compass, your higher self. Your gut is what will lead you and keep you on the path you are meant to be on.

LET'S TALK ABOUT PHYSICS

Isaac Newton was a seventeenth century scientist that discovered the laws of motion. These are very important in our everyday actions as they are the actual scientific basis for how things work. As you read through these laws, they should sound familiar, as you would have once learned them in grade school. However, now as an adult, I would like you to actually read them and understand how they directly affect everything you do.

Newton's First Law: *Every object in a state of uniform motion remains in that state of motion unless an external force is applied to it.* This is also recognized as the law of inertia.

What does this mean for you? Objects at rest stay at rest, and objects in motion stay in motion. Those that stay at rest, stay stagnant and continue to live unhappily and unfulfilled. You need to keep moving to change things. So, time to get moving. Let's talk about the force needed to push you.

Newton's Second Law: *Force equals mass times acceleration (F = ma).* In this law, the direction of the force vector is the same as the direction of the acceleration vector. So, according to Newton, force causes a change in velocity.

What does this mean for you? The size of the mass is the size of your goal. The strength of the force is what will accelerate the mass. So, a big goal requires a strong force. The acceleration is how quickly you can accomplish your goal based on the strength of your force. Simply stated, a little bit of effort produces a little bit of result while a great effort produces a great result.

Newton's Third Law: *For every action, there is an equal and opposite reaction.* This is my favourite one.

What does it mean for you? Let's understand this law by looking at how birds can fly. When their wings push downward, air pushes them upward with an equal and opposite force. So, if we think about hard work, it requires time, energy, persistence, and resilience. Once we put in the work, we reap the benefits. This happens when we exercise. When we run or lift weights, we feel tired, short of breath, weak. When we finish the workout, we feel energized, healthier, stronger. If your goal requires an education, you struggle through the learning process, with balancing work,

HOW TO CHANGE THINGS

life, and school, and with fatigue, stress, and time management. When you finish your program, you have what you set out for. You get to work the job you wanted to work, make more money, and develop the pride and respect you wanted for yourself. See? My favourite law. Sacrifice reaps reward.

We are dangerous when we are not conscious of our responsibility for how we behave, think, and feel.
— Marshall B. Rosenberg

9.

THE THING NOBODY EVER TELLS YOU

WHY EMOTIONAL REGULATION MATTERS

*I*f you cannot control your emotions, you cannot control anything in your life. That is how simple and important this part is. As we learn what emotional regulation is and how to feel all the feels, it comes with a huge learning curve and a whole lot of perspective. People only know what they know, and we all live in our own little worlds. If we can learn to think outside of ourselves, then we can begin to take control of the roller coaster of emotions that constantly runs through us.

This is going to sound so simple, but do you actually know how to recognize each emotion as it comes? Or do you spend most of your time just reacting?

If you are able to pause and do a quick self-check in to recognize every emotion as you experience it, you can learn how to use your emotions as communication tools between your body and your mind, rather than as reactions and outbursts. Nobody likes going from zero to sixty in a hot minute. Regulate yourself to get everything you want out of every situation. Here's how.

1. *Identify how you are feeling*. What emotion is it? Name it. Now ask yourself what caused you to start feeling this emotion?

2. *Take some deep breaths* and allow yourself to feel all the feels of this emotion. Allow all of your thoughts to pass through you like clouds and let them go.

3. *Find a solution*. What will help this emotion pass?

Each emotion you feel is your body trying to tell you something. The crazy thing about our bodies is that we store old emotions from past experiences deep inside of ourselves, so a lot of times when something makes us really mad or sad, it's because it is a trigger from a past experience that our body is trying to warn us of. This is so important! This secret is like gold for anyone in a relationship, for any parent, for anyone trying to be successful in any career... the list goes on. It's honestly life-changing once you can acknowledge this. It does take practise, so if you haven't already tried, it is time to start.

After my dad died, I spent two years in this crazy roller coaster of emotions, and it was then that I learned that I had triggers from all the stuff I had never dealt with in my past very much alive within me. People fighting immediately sent me into an internally anxious state. My chest would tighten and I wouldn't be able to catch my breath. Even people raising their voices or being irritable made me feel so uncomfortable. This became a problem because I didn't actually know what was going on inside of me. And when you don't even know what's wrong, it makes it almost impossible to fix. So, here's where I'd love to give you a heads up on something I had to figure out the long, hard way.

I read a lot of books and talked with my life mentor—my former nursing instructor. She helped validate my emotions, because at the time, I didn't even think I was entitled to feel certain emotions! After years of being made to feel like I should be invisible and just fine all the time, I just went through life thinking my feelings didn't really matter. I felt like I didn't deserve the kind of happiness that some other people had, like I didn't deserve to feel spoiled with love, like I didn't have the grounds to be angry or upset at someone's actions even if they really hurt me, like I didn't deserve to be made to feel special. I needed my nursing instructor to tell me I really did matter and that every emotion I had was valid.

Looking back now, I can't believe I thought so little of myself, but I know I'm not the only one that has. If this is you in any way, you need to keep reading. This book will be life-changing for you, as my mentorship was to me. Everybody needs the proper information and knowledge to succeed in the life they are trying to create, and these lessons just aren't included in the grade school curriculum. Though, I must say, at least in the current curriculum they are naming emotions starting in kindergarten, so here's to hoping our children come out better equipped to graduate into adult life with all the challenges it can bring than a lot of us were.

Emotional regulation requires a lot of internal work for something that should be so simple, but now that I know how to recognize and handle emotions, it has become a simple process. But, it's not always easy to do, so make sure you give yourself lots of grace in this area. The following is the process I came up with for myself after much research and soul searching. You might have to adjust the process to suit your unique needs. It's all broken down into three simple steps.

1. *Name the emotion.*
Yes, it's that simple. Just name it. Look at all of the emotions and name what you are feeling. Having the ability to recognize your emotions is the first step in getting control of them.

2. *Validate the emotion.*
Let yourself know it is OK to be feeling what you are feeling. You must first believe you are worthy of feeling this way, so to that little voice that pops into your mind and tells you that you are being silly and need to get over it, tell it to F off. You must be stern with this voice because it is your ego trying to maintain its tough nature by pushing true emotions back down and burying them. Your ego hates to be vulnerable. Your ego wants you to be tough and to carry on without addressing the real issues that will never go away unless you work through them. Your ego is a protective mechanism, trying to save you from admitting things that hurt you, trying to save your pride. This kind of behaviour works for a while, but eventually everything always comes out. If you don't allow it to get out, if you choose to medicate it instead with alcohol, drugs, pills, sex, or reckless behaviour, it will eventually show up in a physical ailment or disease. You will fall apart one day. No one can be that tough and go on pretending all their life.

THE THING NOBODY EVER TELLS YOU

I'm going to tell you a little more about my grandmother to help you see. This story depicts what happens when you bury emotion and how it spreads toxicity like wildfire to others around you. My grandma is a prime example of a destroyed soul that never gave herself permission to validate her emotions. She never believed she was worthy enough. This beautiful, strong woman endured so much hurt in her childhood, then lost herself in her adult life pleasing and caring for everyone but herself. This beautiful soul that loved me so much taught me to wipe my tears away when the men came in and not to show my emotions. She taught me not to cry. I always thought, *Wow, what an amazingly strong woman she was*, and she was. However, I learned later in life that for years as she had aged, she had started taking anti-anxiety pills to cope with what she had pushed down. Pills and stubborn strength to hide the fact that she was destroyed on the inside.

Every time my dad did something shameful, every time he drank, every time he hurt someone, she would pop another pill. All of her buried anger toward her abusive father and the guilt and shame she must have felt with her own son following in his footsteps—my soul cries for her now that I understand. In her later years, she became ice cold. She lost her ability to show any emotion at all, kept her lips pursed all day, and when I looked into her eyes, I no longer saw her. It was crazy to me. Where had my grandmother gone? The one that had loved me so much. Now she just stared blankly.

My grandfather is a kind and caring man. All my life, I watched him and my grandmother in their married life, respecting each other and living through challenges with what seemed like such grace. Now I'm not so sure they even talked much about the real problems. Then again, I wasn't ever around for any type of emotional sharing in that house or any house in my childhood. It just wasn't a thing any of my family did.

So, what happened to my grandmother's life, just from hiding her emotions? She stopped doing anything and became weak and debilitated once she gave up. She spent years prior to this popping anxiety pills to medicate her true emotions. It eventually killed her.

Hearing the backstory of someone that failed to validate their emotions is what you need to hear to be able to recognize the severe importance of the practice. It shows exactly how our mental health is directly related to our physical health. If you start researching disease, you will start finding people's stories of how cancer and other debilitating diseases show up through stress. Heart attack and stroke in your fifties and sixties is a common thing we see in health care. I ask every heart attack and stroke survivor about their lives, and they all have one thing in common: stress.

The genetic tendencies for these diseases live inside our cells, and when we don't properly take care of our health, they show up. Maybe you survive it, maybe you don't. But your life is never the same once you lose your health. The more and more I study it, the more I understand the direct correlation between mental wellness and physical wellbeing. This is down to even muscle and back pain. You can open your mind to it, or you can call it crazy and continue on as you were. But one day, you'll see.

If everyone believed in this, the universal pain that is so overwhelming in the world would dissipate. We would be left to live more peaceful, content lives full of gratitude and love for each other. Yes, most will say it's all fluffy. But I know you believe me, or you wouldn't have picked up this book in the first place. I know you are one of the few willing to take the time to at least consider how important this "fluffy" stuff is. Stuff as simple as emotions.

3. Feel the emotion.

Another hard step. Validating the emotion is hard because you may not feel you deserve to feel a certain way, but you can be talked through it so that you eventually believe it. Feeling the emotion is hard because it hurts very much to let these emotions debilitate you as they take the time to pass through you. It will feel like your heart is literally breaking. It gets squeezed, you can't take full breaths, and tears can start to pour out of your eyes, so many that you may wonder how your body keeps making them... so many that some days your body actually runs out of them. In these moments, depending on how severe your pain is, it may feel like it will never end, like you may never stop hurting. And in all honesty, you never truly will stop hurting, but time does lessen the severity of the wound. The pain and the scars will never go away, but you can learn to live with the pain and return back to a life you can feel happy in if you are willing and capable to do the work. I believe people are wired to do hard things, so I believe you can do this.

To help draw you a picture of what happens when you don't face your pain, I'll tell you a story about my mom. She forgives everyone for anything they do; a passive and gentle soul sent here to love people for who they are no matter what choices they make. I'm very grateful to have been given to her to raise, because much of her gentle soul is within me. Everything that I am because of her has allowed me to feel so much empathy for people and to forgive them when they make wrong choices.

My mom numbs pain because it's just too hard for her to feel it. That's how she explained it to me one day when I asked her why she kept drinking herself into oblivion. She said it had started years ago when my dad got really mean. He used to do stuff to her that I don't even want to get into in this book. So, to endure it, she would drink until she passed out so that she didn't have to feel it while it was happening. Heartbreaking. Her poor body took all kinds of abuse. Every kind there is.

After my little brother died, she lost herself in the grief, which made it even easier to drink. She said that when she thinks of little Christopher, her baby boy, she can't take the pain so she opens her bottle. As soon as her mind wanders to old memories, down the vodka goes. Numb it. Bury it. Repeat.

The most important thing I have learned along the way in loving a broken person is to always take the good moments and hold much gratitude for them.

When Ty was three years old, we finally talked my mom into moving off the farm and into town after my dad brought his girlfriend home to live with them. For the first time that my mom could remember, she was on her own. Shortly after she moved and found a bit of peace in the safety of not living with my abusive father and his girlfriend anymore, she was diagnosed with muscular dystrophy. No one that she knew of in her family had ever had muscular dystrophy, nor did my brother or I carry the gene for it when we were tested. Just her. Was it bad luck? Or was it years of drinking and stress?

My dad never stopped abusing her. I guess he still needed his fix to relieve his stress, so he stopped in to see her and continued the cycle.

One day, I had a vision while I was working. The phone would ring in the middle of the night, and it would be my brother. He would tell me that our mom was very sick, and that the Doctor didn't think she would make it. This vision and feeling of intuition stayed with me for months, until one night when I was cuddling my son in his little bed. He'd had trouble falling asleep and wanted to have me there, so I laid with him and fell asleep holding him. At 2:00 a.m., the phone rang. I already knew who it was. I calmly answered. My brother told me that our mom wasn't well and that a doctor was riding in an ambulance with her as he wasn't sure she would survive the hour drive to the nearest hospital equipped to treat her. I was a nurse at this hospital, so I woke Ty up and we calmly made our way to my workplace. They called STARS after she arrived as she was actually too sick for their facilities and needed a major city ICU. She was put on a ventilator and survived, but I'll never forget what her doctor said that day. Before he left to go back to the small-town hospital, he told my brother and I that there wasn't much left of my mother's liver, and that if she survived, if she didn't quit drinking then she would not survive the next trip to the hospital.

My brother and I work as a team to care for our mom. I talk to her when she is sober, and I am grateful for those moments. I suggested she move into a lodge to be around more people and receive more support, but we chose to keep her in her own home so she can live her life as she wants. I didn't push for anything more, as after a life of no control in an abusive relationship and all of the losses she has endured, who am I to tell her how to live. Love people where they are at. She doesn't want rehab. Homecare checks on her daily. We continue to love her dearly. Everyone is on their own path.

So, now you can see the importance of feeling the emotion and what happens if you numb it. Enough said.

The idea behind emotional regulation is to not suppress emotions, but rather to learn to manage them. Emotions shape our words and actions, which are the basis for how we react to people and situations in life. To master success in our relationships, career, parenting, and everyday mental wellness, we must learn how to manage our emotions. Emotional intelligence is a huge part of our soul's growth and development, but this accomplishment does not come without the challenges and life experiences that allow us to practise it.

How did I break the cycle? I have no health issues, a healthy relationship with my husband, three beautiful babies and one on the way, and a career in an area I feel passion for. How am I actually living the life I dreamt of and that I love very much? Maybe it's because I'm lucky. Maybe it's because I listen to God. Maybe it's because I've learned how to regulate my emotions.

IN THE MOMENT: PUTTING IT INTO ACTION

There's something we should discuss further when we talk about regulating emotions. It's important to have the knowledge of why we should regulate our emotions and how it affects our health, mental wellness, and ability to get what we want, but it's time now to put that understanding into action. Let's explore the tactical parts of both the external and internal control of emotions in the moments when they rush through, because the actual doing is the hardest part. When you learn how to control emotions in the moment, you find almost immediate relief from the uncomfortable storm, and you learn to get what you want from almost any situation.

When I'm nursing, I have an ability to remain calm on the outside while I work on calming the stress response naturally occurring internally. I wasn't always good at this, but time and experience have led me to develop a stronger ability to be able to calm my thoughts so that I am able to act faster and more efficiently in a crisis. We can't all be acute care nurses in conquering this

THE THING NOBODY EVER TELLS YOU

skill, so I will tell you how else you can do it without applying to nursing school.

In this learning process, I have read a lot of books on meditation and about how to separate the ego of the mind from the inner workings of the soul. It takes practice, but once you conquer it, it's like riding a bike.

People are always saying to me, how are you so calm all the time? When I first started in the ER, the staff kept commenting how calm I was, and when I attended my first code with a new group of co-workers, I received compliments for how calm I was, even from one of the toughest charge nurses. The next day I kept hearing, "You're the new one that was so calm and performed so well in that code yesterday." As for that one cut-throat charge nurse, she approached me another day and asked about my story—where I had previously worked, how long I had been nursing for, etc. We talked for a bit and I quickly learned a lot about her nursing history too. After working with me for a couple weeks, she started going out of her way to ensure I was able to escape for proper breaks, and she continued to have my back going forward. Once people can see potential in you and they know you are not afraid of doing the hard stuff, they grow an almost instant respect for your character. As do I when I meet people.

There is something worth noting about someone that shows courage and faces hard things with resilience. Now, I'm not telling you this to put myself up on any mountain top. I'm telling you this because sometimes you learn things about yourself from the world around you. Things that become reasons for other things. My calm is one of the main reasons I keep getting a constant nag to write this book, actually.

So, I'll tell you the secret in all of this. The truth behind the calm superpower I seem to have developed... I am never as calm on the inside as I seem to be on the outside. In fact, when I first started nursing, I would sweat so much that I'd soak the armpits of my scrub top and my hands would shake every time I was put on the spot. It was horrible.

I am fair-skinned, blond, with blue eyes, and I wear my emotions right there on my face. I turn all sorts of exciting shades of pink and red. And everyone gets to see it.

You can't hide armpit stains and a red face. You just can't. It's why I don't play poker. Sincerity just blasts through my face, and everyone always knows when I'm mad, embarrassed, nervous, or turned on. Ha. Try to be a private person with this problem. Not cool. But! That's me, and I have finally learned to accept this part of me. People laugh at me, but I laugh with them, because in all honesty, it's usually the most entertaining part of a stressful situation.

I'll tell you a little story about my red face. I was working on a surgical unit at the time, and there was an intern who was very handsome. Dark hair, brown eyes, tall, and shoulders so thick you could just wrap yourself up in them. Which I accidently did one day. Here's what happened.

I was standing up at the nursing desk, charting. Everyone was around, including most of the staff that worked on the unit. Mister handsome strutted up carrying a box of muffins and doughnuts and set them beside me. He told me they were a thank you for all our help during his stint at our hospital. I looked up at him and said, "Oh, you didn't have to do that, that's so sweet of you!"

He turned his thick chest toward me and sort of shrugged his shoulders while lifting his arms, as if to say, "It's no problem," however, my immediate take on his body language was that he was motioning for a hug—so I went all in.

In a second, I landed my head right in the middle of his chest and wrapped my arms right around him. I just melted on in there and hung on, until I felt his body stiffen a bit and his hands awkwardly pat my upper back... *Oh shit*, I thought. *He wasn't going in for a hug... He was just shrugging his shoulders!* And now I was stuck there with my head on his chest, and everyone was staring at us.

As soon as I had realized what was actually happening, I could feel the warmth start in my chest, move up my neck, and then boom. Right there in my cheeks. Pink, then red. And then from cheeks to my whole face. I worked up the nerve to release myself and face him and everyone watching. I smiled a polite, pursed-lip smile and turned around to walk into the staff room where I could gather my composure. Everyone stared, jaw-dropped and laughing, and to this day they still have never let me live it down. They assured me my face stayed red for a couple hours afterward, and I just thought to myself, *Wow, I just hope I never see him again.*

Well, I did see him again. The very next day. We met while walking through the short hallway outside the ER doors, and he shrugged up his arms again! I wasn't falling for it this time, so I sprinted past him before he could see my damn face turn shades of pink and red again. I was out of there.

You see? No poker face.

So, now that you have a better picture of how I wear my emotions on my face, let's get back to talking about my sweat stains. Yes, I do still sweat when shit goes down. And when people ask me how I'm so calm all the time, I just smile and say, "I'm not really," and I show them my armpits. I am never as calm on the inside as I seem on the outside, because I'm normal! I'm not a robot and I'm not a superhero. Remaining calm is a superpower though, and I intend to have you develop it by the time you are done reading this book. It will change you. And it will allow you the chance to get what you want.

So how do we maintain external control even while experiencing internal stress? First of all internal and external control go hand in hand. When you can maintain external control it helps to combat the internal physiological responses of the stress response which in turn, helps keep you from entering panic mode. This is beneficial on the effects internal stress has on your body. It helps keep you regulated. Your mind is the like the pilot here. It has control of the whole operating system.

So when you learn to control your external response system, it's looks sort of like pretending at first. The reason external and internal control systems work hand in hand is you start internally which helps reflect your external controls. Here's an example. You are face to face with someone who has just insulted you and you can feel your heart rate start to increase. What follows next? Blood rushes to your head, your brain feels like fog just rolled in and you suddenly can't think straight. You are caught off-guard by the comment and the emotions that have flooded your brain. What's your response? You can't even think of one. You freeze. Or worse. You react. Emotions fly out of you like a plane spinning in the sky. Get a hold of those controls pilot, this spiral can only lead to one thing. Control is key. So we'll start with a deep, long, slow breath. This will combat the stress response spiraling off inside of you so you can clear the fog out of your brain and form a thought for a logical response. It sounds easy when you read it, but we all know how truly hard it is to get control of yourself when your body's stress system takes over. Here's where the pretending comes in.

THE THING NOBODY EVER TELLS YOU

The physiological symptoms of the stress response happen innately because when an alarm sounds we immediately react to find safety. We think we are being chased by a bear. I dig into the details of the stress response in part two, but for now just focus on the task. Once you start to breathe notice your heart rate slow a bit. This takes you from "about to spiral out of emotional control" to "how do I want to handle this". It buys you the few seconds you need to gain back your composure and think. The secret to keeping calm on the outside is responding, not reacting. If you look calm on the outside, your inside will follow suit. Once you gain a few seconds of composure, get control of your mind. Coach yourself in this moment to look unshaken from the outside and respond in a way to assert an acceptance for what you are willing to tolerate. Pretend, even if you are not feeling that calm and logical. If you are unable to calm yourself enough internally to maintain a calm composure externally then state this conversation will be continued at a later time when you are ready to discuss in a logical manner.

Practise makes progress, and remember your internal will follow your external if you train your mind to perform the actions. It gets easier the more you practise it, and if you get really good at it you'll find you can get what you want out of most situations you are in. You can't control the external environment or the actions of the people in that environment, but you can control your own body and the actions within yourself. It's very hard to be upset with the person that is calm and logical.

"And one has to understand that braveness is not the absence of fear but rather the strength to keep on going forward despite the fear."
— Paulo Coelho

10.

MY FAVOURITE BATTLE GEAR

Resilience. One of the most important traits to acquire in life. Simply put, resilience is the capacity to recover quickly from difficulties. It is the ability to be tough. Once you develop resilience, your inner self will trust you and you will in turn develop self-confidence.

Resilience is an acquired trait, one that must be developed through experiencing pain. Pain is universal among resiliency; they go hand in hand. How do you overcome a painful experience? You stand back up. Here's how.

1. *Take control.* You are the writer of your story. You are in control of how your life will go. Circumstances are resistance, not deterring factors of the future. You're the boss. Keith Whitley said it best in "I'm No Stranger to the Rain." Do yourself a favour in the midst of a battle and turn this song up.

2. *Remain value-centred.* Your moral compass is your gut. Listen to it. It is your internal system of values and it gives you purpose, which in turn gives rise to resilience. Write out your values so you can define them. The main few I focus on are as follows: kindness, integrity, authenticity, faith, happiness, respect, and hard work.

3. *Exercise.* You don't just need to trust me on this one—there is extensive evidence for all the things aerobic exercise can do for our brains and for our physical and mental health. You can battle anxiety and depression, protect your heart and lungs, and move emotions. Exercise increases concentrations of neurotransmitters such as serotonin and norepinephrine by stimulating the sympathetic nervous system. The sympathetic nervous system controls our fight-or-flight response, which is our response to stress. Serotonin and norepinephrine are mood enhancers, and they are necessary in battling depression and anxiety. Simply put, exercise helps you feel better.

4. *Recognize your emotions.* Throughout my many battles with life's challenges, I was always drowning in emotions. Wearing your emotions on your sleeve feels good for the good emotions, but it sure is tough for the bad ones. Fear, sorrow, sadness, anger, defeat, frustration... I finally found a way to get a hold of myself. When

you begin to feel an emotion, recognize and define what it is, then logically think yourself out of it. For example, say I'm feeling mad. Recognize and define it: OK, I'm feeling angry because of something someone did. Now, what am I going to do about it? Thinking logically, I'll know I can't solve anything by immediately confronting this person and releasing my anger on them as this would most likely wreak havoc and either cost me a relationship or cause me more emotional feelings of guilt. So, I can take deep breaths. I can take a walk. When I start to cool down, I will think only good thoughts. I will think about things that create settling emotions. Music can help. Then, I'll formulate a plan. We'll dig deeper into this strategy later, but for now, you get the picture. Practise this every day.

5. *Keep perspective.* When the world seems to be spinning out of control, keep perspective of what you are doing and what you have to be grateful for. It is easy to start feeling sorry for yourself. Allow yourself to do this for a short time—like a few hours, or even a whole day if you need. Then stand up straight, take a deep breath, keep your chin up, and keep going.

6. *Develop positive self-talk.* You are your biggest cheerleader. If you are not, you will learn how to become your biggest cheerleader, because without self-motivation and inner coaching, you will not make it through hard times with a successful result. There is a higher self within your soul that will guide you if you quiet down long enough to listen. There is an inner child within you that needs your higher self to protect them and to ensure their safety and love. You can recognize the inner child because it is the part of you that feels fear, that is most

vulnerable, and that holds trauma. You can recognize your higher self as the inner feeling and voice you hear as your conscience. It tells you what is wrong and what is right, keeps you in line with your inner value system, helps you keep your scared inner child company during the dark days, and makes you aware when there is danger nearby. We will discuss this deeper, but the thing you need to know now is that you must learn to talk to yourself during the most trying of times and remind yourself that you will be OK. And no, talking to yourself doesn't mean you are crazy.

7. *Keep your goals specific.* Figure out what your end goal is. Then figure out the steps to get there. Write it all down. Having a visual is key. Every time you complete a step, large or small, celebrate. Treat yourself to whatever it is that fits in your budget and time, something that makes you feel special and cared for. It could be a few hours at a coffee shop with a great book, a nap, dinner out with a loved one or friend, going to see a movie, sex, ice cream, spending time in a hot tub... I could go on. Pick what works for you and do it every time you get closer to your goal.

8. *Express gratitude.* This is something we all don't do enough. It doesn't take much to look around and see just how lucky we are. Recognize your blessings, journal about them, pray for them, love them. The more often you do this, the better you will feel. You cannot feel sadness, anger, frustration, or anxiety at the exact same time as you express gratitude. Period. Try it—it's actually impossible. So, to replace negative emotions with good ones, practise gratitude over and over. It will get easier to uplift yourself.

MY FAVOURITE BATTLE GEAR

9. *Slow down.* Stop living on autopilot. I know you are busy, but you have time to purposefully slow down and take in moments. You can do a lot in even ten seconds. Hug a loved one for ten seconds, kiss your lover for ten seconds, stare at your kids for ten seconds and see the love in their eyes. Make eye contact and give a firm handshake when you say thank you or nice to meet you. You can find many opportunities to take in moments. I did not used to do this enough, but now that I do it more, I am telling you it is life-changing.

Resilience leads to trust leads to self-confidence. Every time you reach a goal, move a negative emotion, handle a situation, or offer a helping hand, you develop trust in yourself. This will turn into self-confidence, and self-confidence will get you anywhere you want to go.

"The greater the difficulty, the more glory in surmounting it. Skilful pilots gain their reputation from storms and tempests."
— Epictetus

11.

ADVERSITY AT ITS FINEST

Our challenges do not define us. However, the way we respond to them does. Always, always listen to your intuition. I'll never forget the day I looked down at the positive sign on that pregnancy test. I had been feeling nauseated every morning, I had been drinking all the pickle juice, and I had gained a noticeable gut. "Take a test," my friends said. "I bet you are pregnant!" All the classic signs, but I was in denial. I fell over when I saw the truth on that stick.

I was nineteen years old. I had just moved to Calgary after hiding away with my mom for three months to help free her from my father's abuse. My dad had been abusive all my life, but after I had moved away to go to college, my younger brother had passed away and my father had become even more dangerous. When my mom finally agreed to leave my dad and go to stay with my aunt and uncle, I moved two hours away to live with a friend in Calgary and try to be a normal young girl. A normal young girl that was now growing a baby.

I had only lived in Calgary for two months at that point. My boss at Pete's Peanut Pub said I could keep my job through the pregnancy and return as soon as I was ready after I had the baby. He even offered to let me rent one of his apartments at no cost until I was able to work again.

The picture of the little baby from my ultrasound left an unimaginable imprint on my heart. He looked like a real baby in there, and he had been doing flips on the ultrasound screen. A real-life, little energetic peanut.

The counselor I was advised to see asked me, "What kind of stressors do you have?"

"Well," I replied, "my parents are both alcoholics, my father is abusive, my younger brother passed away a year ago, I dropped out of college to move home and protect my mom, and now I live here, with a baby in my tummy."

She apologized to me for having to deal with all of this, then kindly advised me, due to the circumstances and abundant amount of stressors in my life, to have an abortion.

I drove home and picked up my mom. We went out to my little brother's grave site and sat in the car. "It's a boy," I told her.

I'd had a vision about six months ago. I was a single mom with a beautiful boy, and we were walking down a quiet path through some trees, holding hands. I was rockin' single mom life in my vision. I was really, really good at it. But why was it all of a sudden real life? This had only been a vision I'd randomly had one day. A day dream.

"I think the best decision for you is to have an abortion," my mom said as tears fell from her eyes.

"I know," I replied. I made the appointment the next morning.

On the day of the appointment, my intuition was screaming. The message was clear. I got up at 7:00 a.m., picked up the phone, and told the lady on the line that I couldn't go through with the abortion. I couldn't get rid of my baby. I told myself I would figure it out and I would be the best single mom anyone would ever know. I promised my boy that day that I would never let him go. I promised him a life of love and safety. I never looked back.

Today, as I write this to you, my boy just left for baseball practice. He's now nineteen years old. His name is Ty. He saved my life.

"Love you Mom," he called. "Can you close the garage door for me?" You bet, my boy. Drive safe.

In the face of adversity, you must stand up tall, hold your chin up, make yourself a promise, and whatever you do, keep that promise. You must look at the road ahead, and no matter what, you must keep walking down the path you know you should be walking down.

Things don't happen to us; they happen for us. You need to know this. You are in this life to build your character. It is the way you face your problems that makes your character. It is the way you settle your problems that develops what is within you.

When I moved to the little city of Camrose, Ty was three months old. I found a small townhouse to rent, and I got a job at a local steakhouse as a server. I started out on welfare. I paid my cousin to watch my baby while I worked Monday through Friday and every Saturday night. I pumped my milk, supplemented with formula, and carried on each day, holding him each night. I worked my way to being the manager of the restaurant, and every time my paycheque got bigger, my welfare cheque got smaller, and I celebrated each small feat. I'll never forget the feeling I had on the day that I no longer qualified for welfare. I was doing well as a restaurant manager and I was very good at the mom life.

When Ty started his first day of grade one, I started my first day of nursing school. I studied by day and waitressed three to four evenings a week. I graduated as a licensed practical nurse in 2011. I worked days and nights, paid babysitters for the evening and night shifts, slept when I could, and loved my boy every single day.

Today, I am married, I have three children, and I have a fourth baby on the way. While I had the second and third babies, I got my nursing degree. I am a mom, a wife, and a registered nurse with a bachelor of science in nursing. I have learned to deal with challenges in many ways, and for some unknown reason, I have an undeniable, intuitive push to tell you all about what I've learned.

So, let's dig a little further into adversity.

Adversity is a state of hardship or difficulty. If there is one thing I've learned about adversity, it is that it's absolutely necessary. It is in the difficulties, trials, and hardships of life that the soul is enabled to rise. When the soul conquers obstacles, it rises stronger, more purified, deepened in intensity, and it becomes more highly evolved. Every experience is part of the pattern of your life, and there are many lessons to learn from each one. If anything, this gives suffering purpose, as Lord knows suffering without purpose would be excruciatingly pointless.

If you ever get the opportunity to read Silver Birch, I would highly recommend it. For those of you that are spiritual, or interested in becoming more spiritual, he offers a great wealth of knowledge that will give you lots to think about. The book I most loved of his is called *Teachings of Silver Birch*. Another must-read to offer a different perspective during trying times is *The Book of Joy* by his holiness the Dalai Lama, Archbishop Desmond Tutu, and Douglas Abrams. For meditating and grounding yourself, Eckhart Tolle is a great teacher. We will discuss meditation for holistic health further in the book. For those that are more biblical, you will find a wealth of knowledge from reading scripture about trying times here on earth and about the strength you can find in reaching God and understanding his purpose and hopes for what we can all become. The story of Jesus and our free will will help you understand that there is more to this life than just us physical beings here on earth.

I have a Christian background, and it has given me the roots I've needed to explore my spirituality when I needed it the most. I nurture my spiritual self through meditation and prayer. Whatever higher power it is you have faith in, it is yours. Finding faith comes at different times in our lives for each of us, but connecting with a higher power and the spiritual world will provide you with an indescribable peace in your heart and soul. For those of you that have felt this, I need not explain any further. For those of you that have not yet felt this, quiet your mind, open your heart, and pray to have your burdens lifted. You will feel an overwhelming peace inside you, and your heart will feel less heavy. Use the strength that comes from this force to strengthen you and give you the ability to stand back up in the face of adversity. This force is your gut, your inner compass, your intuition, your God.

If you don't believe in anything bigger, then you will find that you will struggle most of your life wondering what it's all for. It's all very interesting when you actually slow down to examine things. We will never know all the answers here, but believing in something more holds more power than you might imagine.

Now, let's talk step-by-step how to overcome adversity and the stress it causes.

Adversity comes in all levels. It can be a trying challenge or extreme heartache. The steps you decide to take will be dependent on how fierce your experience is and what works with your body and soul. If you are in the midst of adversity now, you may be in the eye of the storm. If you are not, then think back to a time when you were in that storm and how it felt. Emotions are running high, outlets are open, old trauma and past experiences are triggered, fog is filling your head so you cannot think clearly, overwhelm is taking over.

HOW TO OVERCOME ADVERSITY

1. *Recognize the problem.* What is causing you immediate stress? What are your thoughts consumed with? When something is bothering us that requires a change or fixing, we tend to replay it over and over in our thoughts. What is the situation or person that is causing emotions such as anger, sadness, or fear?

2. *Take deep breaths.* Taking deep breaths slows your breathing, thus slowing your heart rate and activating your parasympathetic nervous system, which is how

the body de-activates the stress response. This is very important.

3. *Clear your mind* by focusing on your breathing. Tell yourself that you are going to be OK. That you will find a solution. That you will survive this. Bring yourself into an awareness of the present moment by wiggling your fingers, then your toes. Take off your socks and ground yourself to the energy of Mother Earth. Feel the grass, ground, or floor of wherever you are. Focus back on your breathing and study how the breath sounds through each inhale and exhale. In through your nose, out through your mouth. This focus on the breath slows the acute stress response, prevents you from moving into panic mode, and clears your head.

4. *Start to review the problem.* Decide if it is something you are able to control or if it is out of your control. If it is something you can control, begin to explore solutions. Come up with ten. Any ten that pop into your mind. Write them down as they come to you. Keep breathing slowly throughout this process. Don't worry about how to accomplish each solution yet. If the problem is something out of your control, move on to the next step.

5. *Recognize and review your emotions.* Identify ten emotions that you are feeling. Write them down. Keep breathing slowly. If tears whelm, let them flow freely; this is your body's way of releasing tension and trauma. If ugly crying and panic breathing start, slow your breathing back down again and let the tears flow without hyperventilating. Visualize the pain of emotion leaving your body with each exhale. This will keep you

in a controlled response to allow a clear mind and a healthy release of emotion. Go through each emotion you wrote down and discuss with yourself, in your head or out loud, why you feel each emotion. Keep breathing slowly.

6. *Once your body feels lighter* after releasing your emotions, begin to further develop each of the ten solutions you created in step four. Start with the first solution you thought of, only this time carry out that idea in your mind. Imagine yourself following through with the idea to resolve the problem and feel the emotions involved in that process. If obstacles come up in your mind's eye as you are imagining this, follow it through by thinking of ideas to overcome the obstacles. Let this story play out in your mind until you feel ready to start the second solution idea. Repeat this process as you go through each of the ten ideas. Take breaks between ideas if needed, it is not necessary to go through all ten stories in your mind at once. Practicing following through in your mind is practice for real time. We all know that once we have been through something once, it becomes easier the next times after, as we recognize the emotions and what is necessary to perform the action. Visualizing how you want it go is a healthy way to use the positive energy associated with this visualization in real time on execution of the plan.

7. *Be kind and gentle* with yourself always, but especially when you are vulnerable. You must treat your inner child and your vulnerable self with amazing grace and lots of love. This is very important to develop self-trust and self-worth. Practise self-care, which is a topic

we will talk about when we explore physical and mental wellness.

8. *Exercise your body.* Go for a walk, a bike ride, a run; lift weights, swim, or do whatever it is that makes you feel good. This will provide an outlet for stress and emotion, as well as increase serotonin and norepinephrine which are your mood enhancer hormones. These help us feel happier, and they help decrease anxiety and depression. Exercise will also increase dopamine, which is a neurotransmitter that plays a role in bodily functions such as movement, memory, motivation, and pleasurable reward. It helps us feel better.

9. *Connect with others.* Reach out to loved ones or others who are going through or have gone through similar situations. This helps us not feel isolated and alone. Talking about your emotions with others is a very important part of surviving adversity. Think of people who you can ask for help and write them down. Think of people who are in your positive support system—people you trust and that you can rely on—and write them down. If no one comes to mind, do not worry—you can handle anything independently with a strong will. A support system however, will help you feel loved and empowered, so if you do have one, please use it. Communicating your situation and emotions honestly will help in bringing these people in. If you want to handle the problem on your own, then you can be your own support system—you can use your inner strength and positive self-talk to continue.

10. *Relax and do things that you enjoy.* Spend time with animals, read a book, go for a nature walk, have coffee with friends, fish, golf, play sports, kiss your kids. I don't know what makes you feel better, but try these things or do what you already know you love to do. This is important in the healing process as you work through challenging times.

11. *Keep your thoughts positive.* Perform gratitude checks as often as you need them. Make a promise to yourself to do the above listed tasks to better your health, and do not break it. So if you promise to exercise three times in the coming week, make sure you follow through to not let yourself down. Quite like we strive to be dependable at our workplace or reliable to our family members or friends, we should learn to be dependable to ourselves.

Keep going. Look forward. One day at a time, one moment at a time. Soon the clouds will lift, sunshine will appear, and hope will settle in. Quite a storm. Now the person you are after the storm will never be the same.

PART 2

Building a better, stronger you

"The greatest weapon against stress is our ability to choose one thought over another."
— William James

12.

GETTING TO KNOW YOUR BODY

You know the fight-flight-or-freeze response? That known stress response triggered in our bodies when we feel we may be in danger? I used to freeze a lot. It's a natural defence system, like something that might happen if you were chased by a bear... or an elk!

I went camping in Banff one time with my best friend when we were about ten years old. We were out hiking when all at once, this giant elk with the biggest antlers came running up over a hill. He stopped and stared at us for a second, then started chasing us. We were terrified. My friend's amazing body reacted by hauling ass—she burned down that road faster than I had ever seen anyone run before. Me? Not so much. My body chose to freeze. Dead in my tracks, with one foot in front of the other, arms frozen in a running position, jaw dropped, eyes opened wide. My friend kept yelling, "Run Dena!" as she continued hauling ass out of there and back to camp, but my feet were completely frozen to the ground! I could hear her words, but I couldn't move any part of my body. And then it happened. The pee started coming. The elk was charging and my pee was pouring out. My body hadn't moved from its mid-run position, but my pants were soaked.

Well, I'll tell you, that elk ran right up to me, stopped about four feet away, and stared. I swear he knew I had peed my pants. I actually think he felt sorry for me. Then he turned around and walked away. Just like that. Holy Christ was my heart pounding. My superhero-response friend was long gone by then. I walked back to camp, checking behind me every few seconds to make sure the elk wasn't following me, and doing that bowlegged cowboy walk you do when there's pee in your pants.

I showed up at camp as my friend was anxiously reporting what had happened to her family. She was telling them that they needed to go and see if the elk had gotten me. As I approached, they looked up to see me in one piece before glancing down at my pants. The effort they made to hold back their smiles was top-notch. They asked if I was OK, tiny giggles hiding under their words. My friend was still pale with disbelief and wonderment that I actually made it out alive.

Honestly, this was one of the scariest things that could ever happen to someone hiking in Banff! Well, I thought so anyway. But I'll never forget how amazing my awesome friend was to respond so effectively, and I will never forget how my response wasn't so effective that day. So, you can see how the fight-flight-or-freeze response can serve you (or not) in your life.

Time to get all nurse-y on you.

THE STRESS RESPONSE

When you first sense danger, your sympathetic nervous system initiates an acute stress response in your body. Our bodies were designed with this stress response so that we could try to survive the stressor. So, if you come across an elk, your fight-or-flight response is designed to allow your body to attempt survival. In my case, apparently, it just likes to make me freeze, pee, and hope that the dangerous thing just doesn't see me.

When your brain sends a distress signal the adrenal glands respond by releasing a combination of hormones to initiate the stress response and to maintain the level necessary to survive the threat. Epinephrine (also known as adrenaline) is the first to be released after the distress signal is sent from the brain, causing the initial physiological effects in your body that are designed to allow you the greatest chance of surviving. Your pupils dilate to increase visibility and focus, your heart rate increases to pump blood to your organs which increases motor function and muscle capability, your respiratory rate increases for greater oxygen intake, and your digestive system slows or dumps what it is currently trying to process (so we become nauseated, vomit, have diarrhea... or pee) to preserve the energy required to fight or run. Epinephrine triggers the release the glucose and fats from storage sites to allow an increase of nutrients into the bloodstream, which supply energy to all of your body systems, giving us the extra energy in survival mode. It's the adrenaline rush you all are familiar with. Epinephrine is a short acting hormone, so after it subsides the body goes through a cascade of other hormones producing what we all know as cortisol. Cortisol is known as the stress hormone. It is what keeps your sympathetic nervous system running. It keeps you in fight or flight. Your body releases cortisol when you are in an acute stress response, traumatic stress response, and chronic stress response. In the acute and traumatic response it keeps you on high alert. It releases sugar from your liver for fast energy and keeps you in survival mode.

This acute stress response is the same whether we meet a bear, have a confrontation with someone, receive news that someone we love has been hurt or has passed away, are verbally or physically abused, are in a situation that we feel is out of our control, encounter a risk to our health or wellness, face a threat to the safety of ourselves or loved ones, or sense potential danger in any form. It is designed to protect us.

This acute stress response turns into a chronic stress response if the problem or stressor is not removed and our bodies continue to function in the fight-or-flight mode. This becomes detrimental to our health. Stress affects every body system and every organ. It is especially hard on the cardiovascular system and digestive system, and it creates almost all disease, including mental health issues.

The point of all this health education is that we must learn to control stress in order to maintain health and wellness. If we learn to control stress in a healthier ways, we become healthier humans. We become better mothers and fathers, better husbands and wives, better sons and daughters, better friends and colleagues... better people.

First and foremost, we must learn to listen to our bodies. Recognize when you enter into this acute stress response. Notice the physical changes that happen in your body. Then figure out why you are in this response. What is it that your body is sensing that is causing you to feel nervous, scared, angry, or sad? This is a direct cue from your insides, a clear communication from your soul that has activated your brain and asked you to react. It could be a trigger from something your soul recognizes from the past, an immediate danger from someone about to cause harm, or an underlying fear of something that you feel will affect your safety. The way you respond is a map to what the problem might be.

For me, I have always had trouble speaking my true feelings to people in fear of hurting their feelings or having them respond negatively. I have been uncomfortable with confrontation all my life, and when I was able to relate this to past triggers, it made a lot more sense.

In the past, whenever someone said something that upset me, it felt a lot more comfortable for me to accept it and discuss it later with a safe friend, or to just bury it and try to forget it. Dealing with the person responsible for upsetting me was too scary. If I attempted to partake in communication with anyone that had upset me in any way, especially those with type A personalities—strong, confident, aggressive in nature—I would freeze again. I never peed my pants, but I definitely froze. My heart would pound inside my chest, my heart rate would increase, my breathing would become more shallow and rapid, my body (like every body part) would start sweating, and blood would rush to my face, leaving it flushed and heated.

Mel Robbins explains a helpful way to slow or stop the body's acute stress response in her book, *The 5 Second Rule*. In her life findings, taking five to ten seconds to slow down your breathing helps to slow the stress response and prevent a panic attack from forming. It also allows you a chance to clear your head and process your thoughts. From a medical point of view, slowing your breathing activates the parasympathetic nervous system, which returns your body systems to their natural resting states after a stressor has gone. It was while reading her book that I was able to realize that my present response to confrontation was connected to trauma I held from my past regarding my safety when my aggressor became aggressive. Another light bulb.

Silence. Silence was my defence mechanism triggered from my childhood to keep me safe, because in my experience, when you spoke to an aggressor, you got hurt. But, somewhere along the way, I lost my voice in the effort to save myself from getting hurt. I froze again and again, and I tried to make myself invisible in order to avoid danger and prevent pain—just as I had reacted to the elk.

Can you relate to this? I mean, maybe you have never peed your pants as an elk chased you, but have you ever lost your voice? Do you clam up and become anxious and panicked when someone is mean to you or when you're confronted? Do you freeze? Words just leave your brain, or your brain knows what it wants to say, but the words get stuck in your throat and nothing comes out. Then later, you find yourself rehearsing everything you wanted to say in your car by yourself, just giving it to that person now that they are no longer there, your chest puffed up, chin held high. The words confidently spew out of you, and you think, *If I could redo this situation, this is what I would say*. It makes you feel better, doesn't it? Well OK, you asked for a redo, so when another situation comes up... the same thing happens again! And there you go in the car again, just giving it to that empty air. And repeat. See? A learning lesson. The same thing, three times or more? It's because of you.

When you are unaware of what is happening, it is impossible to control a natural reaction. Maybe your reaction isn't silence and freezing. Maybe it's anger. If you become instantly angry—chest pounding, fists clenched kind of angry—you are reacting to the possibility of needing to employ the fight response as defence against your aggressor. Again, this response is designed to keep you alive. My awesome friend that ran her ass off away from that elk reacted with flight for survival. If you do the same, then maybe your natural defence is to run away from other aggressors too. Maybe you cannot stand to stick around for confrontation, or you run away from your problems and just hope they dissipate on their own.

When you find out what you are actually doing and what is actually happening and you face the truth, you can begin to unpack it and move toward creating a new natural reaction. You can get a handle on those quick-to-show-up emotions, bringing that wave of anger down before it builds from your feet to the top of your head, stopping yourself from running away from something you truthfully want to address, simmering your acute stress response, and finding your voice again.

Here's a little more about how I found mine again.

"Fear is excitement without the breath."

— Gay Hendricks

13.

FINDING YOUR VOICE

PILLOW TALK

I was first introduced to meditation when I was in my early thirties. The idea of quieting yourself and slowing your breathing was weird to me. I had read a book on how to meditate, how to let go of your controlled thoughts, and the benefits of this practice on your mental wellbeing and physical health, and I thought, *If the practise of meditaton is so minuscule, but the benefits on your health are so extensive, why not try it?* I also kept hearing about how many people who were successful in their careers and life goals meditated, but it was after I read *The Book of Joy* by his Holiness the Dalai Lama, Archbishop Desmond Tutu, and Douglas Abrams, that I was sold. The stories these men hold are incredible. Their ability to forgive, find peace in the midst of a storm, and show so much love to people everywhere is amazing to me.

I have always been a calm spirit by nature, however as I entered into my thirties and began viewing the world and the people in it from a different perspective, studying the behaviours and actions of people on a deeper level, and forming new life goals and dreams for myself, I began to change. After my family expanded and I dove deeper into my nursing career, I began to feel an anxiety inside myself that I did not recognize. I mean, some of the things I had experienced in my younger years and in my twenties had been crazy, yet I had handled each situation as it had come. But now, I found myself feeling anxious about little day-to-day happenings and striving more for perfection in my day-to-day life and nursing activities. It was like now that I had finally reached a point in my life where things were more secure, predictable, and stable, I was terrified to lose it.

The first few times I sat down on my floor, legs crossed, pillow on my back to meditate, I interrupted myself every few seconds. My thoughts were rushing through—my to do list, something someone had said that had made me mad, the form I had forgotten to fill out for Esmee's school field trip, what I should make for supper, why my past felt so heavy, how I should deal with the constant guilt I was feeling for finally pulling away from years of trying to get my parents sober, what kind of clothes I wanted to buy for my birthday, what had happened with a patient I'd been with earlier that week, how to raise a teenager that had suddenly stopped telling me everything about his life, how out of touch I had become with God, what I was going to write that paper about for my nursing course, if I had given the kids enough attention that week, if I should set aside a date night with my husband so we could be with each other away from the business of life, the nerve of that person to say those rude things to me... the list could honestly go on for pages. I know you know! We all have thousands of thoughts a day, some fleeting, some productive, some emotional, some reflective, some worrisome. And honestly, once you have a spouse and little people that rely on you, some days the thoughts just build up at such an incredible pace that it feels like you will never catch up.

This is where meditating comes in. When the thoughts enter your mind, I find it helpful to think of them like clouds passing by on a breezy day. The thoughts arrive, I acknowledge them, and then I let them pass by.

Every thought deserves acknowledgement, just as every emotion deserves validation. It is through thought acknowledgement that you can start to reflect on why you might be feeling certain things, and how your thoughts might connect to other things in your past or your future visions. If you recognize a connection, allow yourself to feel the emotion that comes with it, let it pass by, and then move on to the next.

Once you practise this enough times and are able to control those fleeting thoughts and reach a relaxed state in your brain, amazing things really do happen. You will begin to receive what feels like absolute truths to questions you have been wondering about, explanations to problems you have been facing, validation for emotions you have been feeling. All of a sudden, you'll come out of this trance, and your brain will feel more rested than it ever has before. Your body will feel calm and relaxed, and you will have received an interesting message or seen an interesting vision through your thoughts that will give you something new to ponder about and to try and figure out.

Meditation really is soul healing. But, it truly is a practice, and it takes dedication to ensure that you are doing it enough to get better at it, just like anything else you have ever tried to improve at. So, whether you have five minutes, twenty minutes, or an hour, take the time to practise slowing your thoughts and finding quiet in your brain. It truly is incredible for your mental health and for improving efficiency in the busy life you are trying to lead. It is how I eventually gained the calmness back in my gut.

HOLISTIC HEALTH AND NATURAL HEALING

Have you ever heard of Reiki? Are you familiar with energy movement in our bodies, with chakras and unlocking blocked energy centres? If you haven't heard of Reiki, or if you don't know much about it, I would strongly suggest you to open your mind and study the art of this practice in consideration for natural healing. My whole belief centre around nursing is a holistic approach to wellness: mind, body, and soul, as they are all connected. Mental health and wellness directly affects our physical health.

Science is amazing, and so is old traditional healing if you are open to believing in it. If you believe in both, I feel you have many options to explore. I do, however, very strongly feel that the root cause of both emotional and physical problems should be addressed, if at all possible, rather than just making a quick jump to medicinal treatment. This of course excludes cases of the many disease processes that require medication to alleviate life-threatening aspects of system failures.

My first experience with Reiki goes a little something like this. I had just given birth to my daughter and as you know, life doesn't stop for you when that baby lands. We had family staying with us, a dog that came along with them that loved chewing up our clothes and the baby's poopy diapers, lots of other family and friends stopping in to meet baby, and my son was in hockey so we were at the rink the day after baby was born. I didn't want to miss his life just because I had a new life that needed me, and I didn't know what rest was during this time. I was working on my degree days before the baby landed and I loved to do it all.

Alone time? Who needed it. I was OK. I could do it.

Damn, those dishes were never ending and the laundry was piled up. The house was a disaster and there were so many people in the house to take care of. We had kids and dogs and extra family staying with us and I was struggling trying to keep up with the meals. My boobs were engorged and baby was having trouble latching on to what seemed to be size triple Z, the sutures from my torn vagina were sore, and things were leaking out of every orifice. I had a hard time asking for help. I didn't want to seem bossy, or to become a nag. I felt so alone, and overwhelmed. As time kept moving along, new challenges would pop up day by day.

But one day, I came across a person who lied to me. Have you ever met someone who could chronically lie? Like, could looked you in the face and blatantly lie to you, unashamed? I find these types of people interesting now, but back then I found them infuriating.

Honesty is something I value, even though at that time I also wasn't being honest with people about how I was feeling. I preferred to hold the pain to myself, rather than inflict it on others. I believed that if I told others how I was feeling, they would feel bad about how they had made me feel, which would cause them to feel shame, and I had seen enough shame and sadness in my parents' faces all my life that I didn't want to create more in anyone else. I made the choice to keep my feelings hidden in order to make things easier on others. But when people told blatant lies for their own gain? That really bothered me. I couldn't stand it.

Considering everything I'd had on my plate, this one conversation with a liar just left my head tilted, jaw dropped, with no idea what to even say or where to go from there. It had put me over the edge in my lack of ability to speak. I felt like a tornado was inside of me, swirling and circling and about to explode out of me. I felt that everlasting lump in my throat, my heart pounded, my chest felt tight. It was an I-don't-even-know-what's-happening-here kind of feeling. But I knew I needed to fix it. So, I made an appointment with a woman that did Reiki, which I had heard was a really effective stress management technique.

Wow, the woman was calming. I felt so good just being in the same room as her, and we hadn't even talked yet. I told her I was there for stress management. She instructed me to lay on the sheet on the bed and to close my eyes. She started on my stomach. She didn't directly touch me, just hovered her hands over me. I started to feel warm in the spot she was hovering over. Every time she moved her hands, the heat would follow. Without much delay, she came right up to my head and neck. She stayed on my neck. She told me she felt a lot of tension in the area and that she would spend most of the hour there, with her hands moving calmly and quietly around my shoulders, neck, and throat. It felt so warm and relaxing the whole time I laid there. She finished at the bottoms of my feet. I felt very relaxed, but not that much different from when I'd come in. My head felt heavy and my throat still felt blocked, like that lump was still there, but somehow it was like it had spread out more so that it wasn't quite as uncomfortable. It was enough that I decided to book another appointment with her. She advised me that it might take a few sessions before I really felt anything change, depending on my belief system and how open I was to receiving the treatment.

FINDING YOUR VOICE

On the second visit, she once again started at my stomach. That time, she took her time there, moving her hands to hover over my heart, down my arms, then back to the top of my head. I could feel the heat more intensely this time in each area she worked on. I felt a swirling motion inside my body where she hovered and circled her hands, and this time when I closed my eyes, my mind fell into peace and silence. My thoughts went quiet and I found myself in the farmhouse bedroom I grew up in. It was like a movie was playing in my mind. The walls were a familiar light pink and there was a little blond girl sitting cross-legged in the middle of the floor by a bed, right where I used to sit and play. The quilt on the bed was the same pink, quilted blanket my grandma had made me, with pink threads coming out of each perfectly sewn knot. I used to run my fingers through those silky threads over and over. It used to bring a sense of calm in my chest and my stomach.

The little girl was playing with a blond-haired Barbie. She was looking down at the Barbie so I couldn't see her face. I got the feeling that she was about four or five years old. I could feel that she was scared and lonely. It was really quiet in the room, but there was a lot of muffled noise and voices coming from outside the room, travelling down the hall from the living room and kitchen. She froze.

Then, like someone had grabbed me and quickly pulled me backward out of a blurry tunnel, I started and my eyes flew open. I gasped for a deep breath upon waking. Holy shit. I felt so disorientated for a few seconds. When I'd come to, my Reiki healer had still been at my head, and I had felt a radiating warmth over my neck and the top of my head. I continued to breathe deeply as she wound her way back to my stomach and down to my feet.

When the session finished, I told her about my dream. She explained that some people called these "visions," and they

137

were brought out through the subconscious mind. Sometimes they were past supressed memories, or in some cases they were glimpses into future moments. I knew right away that I had been the little girl. I had felt all of her fear and loneliness. My heart ached for her. I don't know what happened to her when she was that little, or what had happened that day in her room, but I'll never forget how it had made me feel in the present time. As I drove home that day, I had a whole new perspective on how I felt about myself. I looked at myself with the same compassion I felt for that scared, fragile little girl that needed safety and comfort, and I promised myself, with everything in me, that my children would never feel that way in their lives. I would make sure of it.

A few days after that Reiki session, I began to express to my husband how I had been feeling since the baby had been born. How I needed to have space in the house to be alone sometimes, how I needed help with day-to-day chores, and how that session had made me feel so vulnerable. He listened to me talk and expressed his annoyance at me for allowing things to get this stressful when all I had to do was say something before it got so bad. He truly didn't understand when I said I couldn't just say how I was feeling for fear of hurting others' feelings. He began helping with tasks around the house, and I worked on practising asking for help when I felt I required it. Teamwork was such a simple solution, yet it felt so impossible in the midst of it.

My husband was astounded by my vision in the Reiki session. He grew up around a Native community in beautiful British Columbia, so he had been introduced to natural healing and spirit cleansing when he'd been a teenager. He told me some stories of what some of the local Natives would do during healing ceremonies and we talked about all kinds of crazy things like astral travel and soul exploration. These were things I hadn't even known existed, but that I had still experienced years ago after losing my younger brother. I found it all very fascinating.

The Reiki healer had spent so much time on my throat and neck because my voice had been lost. This was the start of me finding it again. I had had neck pain for a couple of years prior to these events. I had changed my pillows and gone to a chiropractor routinely to get my range of motion back so that I could at least turn my head comfortably enough to work and function day-to-day. After Reiki, my neck pain went away, the lump in my throat dissipated, my chest felt a little less tight, and my anxiety started to settle. That is, until August 2018. Then I received a phone call that changed everything inside of me again.

LEARNING TO SPEAK

My family and I were on holidays, hanging out in the beautiful Okanogan while visiting my husband's grandfather. We were off to Kangaroo Creek Farm when my brother called. My dad had unexpectedly passed away. My brother had gone over to bring him tomatoes and had found him laying on the floor next to his bed.

My dad had been fifty-eight years old, but he'd looked seventy. His health had been deteriorating slowly, and he'd had back, hip, and joint pain, along with every other problem that could be connected to the hepatic system. Years of abuse on the liver affects more than you can imagine, especially if you've never studied disease processes or body systems. Nobody really ever sees the compound damage they do to themselves with unhealthy habits until it manifests as a physical ailment or disease.

A few days before we had left to go camping through the beautiful lakes and mountains of British Columbia, I had been driving home from work when I got a sudden slam of insight: someone I loved very much was going to die very soon. I had never experienced this before, but I knew that what I had felt was so strong, I couldn't ignore it. I thought right away that it must have been about my grandmother. She had been weak and not feeling well for a while, and I hadn't had the time in my bustling life to see her as often as I used to.

I was shaken by this overwhelming feeling of impending doom, so I pondered cancelling our holiday and staying close to home in case something happened to someone. After talking it over with my mom, I allowed myself to go ahead and enjoy our family holiday. We really only got to escape once a year, and family time to be together without the bustle and business of life was so important to my soul. So, I went. And when my brother called, I was blown away. Firstly, because my intuition had forewarned me about this, but secondly, because I'd had no idea that it would be my dad. So many things came rushing into my brain, including all of the things I had never had a chance to say to him (I had spent my life up until then with no courage of voice).

My family and I all piled into the vintage '88 motorhome we took camping each year, and as we made our way back home, memories and emotions flooded me. It was a good twelve hours where I sat, watched the mountains pass by, and cried. I let the thoughts flow in and the emotions overtake my heart. One thing I had never realized was that when you lose a parent, as those of you that have know, it's like your roots get ripped out from under your heart, creating a loneliness you never expected. All your life, you have been attached to this person, this person who created you, this person who was the reason you were even brought into this world—even if they weren't always that nice to you.

After the adrenaline rush that allows you the strength to plan a celebration of life and attempt to start to find a way to say goodbye to someone who has passed, things get quiet. It is in this quiet stage that your heart really gets ripped apart. The only thing left for you to do is to grieve your loss, to say goodbye to this person you knew and loved all your life, and in my case, to finally deal with the whirlwind of emotions I had never dealt with in the past, which were now spiraling so out of control that I couldn't run from them anymore. It was like a crazy storm had rolled in, and the only way to settle it was to release it. And so it began.

As life kept moving along, I was commuting to work two hours a day. My drives were filled with flashbacks, tears, confusion, anger, sadness, loneliness, fragility, reflections, audiobooks, songs, and more tears. I would get to work, park, wipe my tears, do the nurse things, leave, drive, think, cry, park, wipe my tears, do the mom and wife things. Life was still manageable in this state. I was meditating, having crazy visons and intuitions about questions I felt I needed answers to, and I was surviving through the initial stages being a broken daughter grieving for her father. The adult in me knew that I simply needed to work through the emotions that everyone experiences when they lose someone, but the little girl inside me was not OK.

I have never in my life felt as vulnerable as I did in that first year after my dad died. I needed support for my broken heart and extra love and validation that I was worthy enough to be loved. Like every daughter that has been abused by her father, my self-worth was just missing. At first, I tried to give myself extra love, support, and validation through my own thoughts and self-talk, as well as through songs. My closest friends were amazing to talk to also, but I didn't like to burden people with negative, depressing, dark stuff, so I mostly just pretended outwardly that I was fine and moving along.

About six months after my dad passed, my brother started acting unlike himself and it became almost too much to handle. He was grieving in his own way and as I lost the support I had in him, the more I looked to my husband to fill the void of self-worth and love I had in my heart and soul. I couldn't communicate to my husband what I needed from him, I just began to see all of the things he wasn't giving me, and all of the things I knew I deserved. After months of this, I had absolutely had enough. That little girl inside of me needed someone to stand up for her, and oh boy, did I ever stand up.

It was like a monster of fury exploded out of me. I cornered my husband one day in the laundry room after numerous failed passive attempts to try to communicate with him, searching for validation of how I was feeling. I told him that he was going to start listening to me. He was going to close his mouth, not say a word, and listen to me until I was finished speaking. He was going to hear my words and acknowledge my emotions, the way every person deserves to be acknowledged. I told him that I mattered, that I was worthy of being loved and supported, and that if he wasn't able or willing to listen to me, then I wouldn't stay there any longer.

Now, the unfortunate thing for my husband that day was that my words were not just meant for him. They were also directed at everyone else in my life that had previously dismissed me or taken advantage of my passive, forgiving nature. But, he finally listened to me.

It. Felt. Amazing.

I had found my voice. And it was never to be lost again.

Luckily for me, my husband was receptive, and for the first time, without his strong personality overruling any conversation or discussion the way it had in the past—he listened to me. He finally let me express my feelings and did not dismiss the fact that they were real and that they meant something. My husband loved me, this much I knew, but what I didn't know then was just

FINDING YOUR VOICE

how much. The simple act of letting me speak without arguing with me about the expression of my emotions was enough to make me feel loved and validated in worth. That's it. That's all I'd ever needed. To be heard. To be allowed to take up space in someone's life to talk and be heard. That's it.

When you become sure about something, you find your confidence and you find your true strength. After that, you earn your own trust, which gives you the peace and serenity of knowing that no matter what, you will be there to support yourself. You will be strong enough to stand up to anyone you are required to, to find solutions to any of your future problems, and to always treat yourself with kindness and grace. It is here, through finding your voice, that you find your self-worth.

"There is no passion to be found in settling for a life that is less than the one you are capable of living."
— Nelson Mandela

14.

THE ONE PERSON YOU NEED

This part of the story is about you. The life you have has one writer. The one person you need, first and foremost, is *you*, because you are the only one you can truly depend on.

Now that may sound negative or like a comment surrounded by black clouds, but I can assure you these words are not spoken out of spite or resentment in any form. These words are spoken out of what I have absolutely learned to be true, and in it will be what first saves you.

In every great love story, the prince always rescues the princess, and in those classic action movies, the big strong hero always saves the people. This will ring true throughout your life also—you will find people that will absolutely save your soul, you will find your own heroes that will save you, and you'll end up being the hero that saves someone else.

But before anyone can save you, you have to save yourself.

You have to be the one that can pick yourself back up when you've fallen, climb out of whatever hole you've fallen into, and claw your way back up the mountain. The reason why this is an absolute truth is because you can't change anyone else, nor can you control the actions or thoughts of anyone else. You only have control of your thoughts, your actions, your perspectives, your emotions, your goals, and your dreams. You do not get to decide how anyone else's story goes, therefore you cannot rely on anyone else to save you or protect you.

This is a very harsh lesson to learn, and for those of you that have had to learn it on your own, I am sorry for the heartbreak that must have come along with that. For those of you that are feeling surprised at these words and are finding a new perspective in them, listen intently. Once you figure out how to make yourself whole, then you can start inviting people that make you an even better person into your life. These people are the ones that make you feel loved and supported and satisfy our human need for companionship and belonging. The difference here is that they will add to your life and your happiness, but you will not be reliant on them for it.

To help you achieve your journey to self-worth and self-reliance, I'm going to dig into a little nursing school education and bring your attention to Maslow's hierarchy of needs. This hierarchy will give you a better understanding of the process of human fulfillment and why becoming self-reliant is so important. Some of you might be familiar with this theory, but for those that aren't,

THE ONE PERSON YOU NEED

Abraham Maslow was a psychologist that developed a human motivational theory that defined basic human needs as a hierarchy, a progression from physical needs for basic survival to more complex emotional needs to complete human fulfillment. The needs are as follows:

- *Physiological* – need for oxygen, food, water, and rest. Everything a human physically needs to survive.
- *Security and safety* – need for shelter and freedom from harm or danger. This entails a sense of security, stability, and order.
- *Love and belonging* – need for affection, the feeling of belonging, companionship, and meaningful relations with others.
- *Self-esteem* – need to be thought of well by oneself and by others.
- *Self-actualization* – need to be self-fulfilled, to learn and create, and to understand and experience one's potential and capabilities.

This theory teaches that the motivational behaviours of humans innately start with survival needs first, before they work to accomplish the next step of the pyramid, and then the next, in order. The idea is that once all these needs are met, you can sit in self-actualization and look back upon your life happenings, feeling complete and fulfilled in your human experiences. It is within the self-actualization stage that you spend the rest of your time, and from there you are able to teach others what you learned to help you reach this stage of fulfillment and contentment.

The really amazing thing about Maslow's theory of human motivation and behaviour is the paradigm shift that was instigated after his discovery. A new definition of positive mental health found that humans are not simply blindly reacting to situations, but rather trying to accomplish something greater. Advances in neurology are confirming that the physiological wiring in the human brain seeks self-transcendence as well as survival. Abraham Maslow and Albert Einstein later studied the characteristics of a self-actualized person. They found that these "special" people were spontaneous and creative, had a clear sense of what they found to be true about life and situations, tended to focus on problems outside of themselves, and experienced moments of what were called "extraordinary" sudden feelings. These were feelings of intense happiness and well-being, joy and excitement, awareness of a higher truth, and intense feelings of love. These extraordinary moments were often inspired by meditation, exposure to music or art, or the overwhelming beauty of nature. The uplifting, soul-transcending experiences of these people affirms that through these activities is indeed where we find our purpose, meaning, and value in existence.

This is exactly where you want to be. In a place where you have self-fulfillment to the point where you can start to really appreciate those little things in life. So now when people say, "Stop and smell the roses," or, "Look around at the beauty that surrounds you," you'll know exactly what they mean. The goal is clear. Let's work through those levels. Thank you, Abraham.

Think about this for a minute and relate it to your own life: if you are worried about feeding yourself or your family, then you will not be concentrating on building self-esteem. Furthermore, if you are in pain, then you will not be focusing on interpersonal relationships or finding love. Or, if you are in danger of someone hurting you, then you will be in survival mode, trying to meet the first levels of physiological and safety needs. Our bodies and souls will perform amazing things to help us survive. One thing to always remember though is that every person is unique in their strengths and ability to cope and survive, which is back to why we can only control our own actions and abilities.

So, where are you in Maslow's hierarchy of needs? What level are you presently working on completing? Once you can see where you are, then you'll be able to see which levels are next for you. This will give you direction in answering the question, what is the purpose of your life? Most people find the purpose of their lives in self-actualization. This comes after finding a sense of belonging in the world by connecting to the people that make them feel loved and cared for, and after finding self-esteem, through which they have developed respect for their bodies and emotions, found a sense of confidence in the person they are and the character of self they are developing, as well as found esteem from others around them.

The whole process brings up nature (the character of self) versus nurture (the effects from the people and environments around us) gain, which relates to all aspects of our development. We can sometimes get lost between nature and nurture when finding ourselves on our life journeys, so looking at the levels of human needs for motivation and fulfillment allow us to answer many questions when dealing with our own character development while also trying to understand the actions of others.

Wherever you are in your life, you need to be the one person you can rely on. So, how do you become independent? How do you change your mindset from needing other people to being your own saviour, first and foremost? Well, first you need to develop trust in yourself. To develop trust in yourself, you need to start making promises to yourself and keeping them. This can start with anything you want to change—anything to do with self-improvement in regards to physical or mental health, anything you want to achieve, anything you think your heart desires. You'll often see that these promises line up with where you are on the hierarchy of needs.

For example, for some, the promises will be about survival—finding safety from your abusive relationship, making enough money to pay your bills and feed your family, making it on your own if you have no family and are in an unsafe situation, battling extreme depression. Whatever it may be, you must first meet these survival needs. If you are in level one or two of the hierarchy, you must gain the strength to start building trust here. Be resourceful in finding solutions—when you get quiet enough, you will start to hear answers. Once you begin to get ideas for how to improve survival, start to figure out a plan of action. You must first think of the end before you start at the beginning, so visualize what safety will feel like through the lens of whatever you are battling. Use professional resources and friends or family members that you feel you can trust to help you. When you are amidst a storm, remember that you cannot see the sunshine even if it is on the way, so you must promise yourself to stay strong and keep going until one day, that light appears. Then hope and relief will set in, and you'll be able to breathe. Keep visualizing that moment. Don't give up.

It's important that through any struggle, any storm, you are your own support coach. Hear me out on this—you are not crazy to talk yourself through it. You have a very fearful and vulnerable inner child that very much needs your protection. Your inner child needs to feel safe or you will never find peace inside.

I talk to myself all the time and it has helped me through every situation I have ever been in. In the moments I need to hear it, I literally tell myself that I'm OK. I tell myself that this will pass, I will be fine, and I will come out stronger after I'm through it. I remind myself to breathe. This helps to bring my heart rate down and it helps me escape the acute fight-or-flight response that can otherwise spiral into a panic attack. I literally self-soothe and coach myself through.

Now be honest and admit that you already do this. Every person has said words of encouragement or support to themselves at some time in their lives. You will recognize it because it's the same voice you hear when you criticize yourself and tell yourself you are not good enough. This is just a nicer you, a much more supportive you. Once you practise this, it will come as naturally to you as the negative thoughts you tell yourself now. The stronger you get, the more you start to love and trust who you are. You'll be able to stop that criticizing self, and you will develop a greater self-worth.

If you don't often say supportive words to yourself, you must start this practice immediately. Once you start, you will begin to recognize this voice and you will learn to trust it. It is your soul. Once you push your ego aside, you make room for your higher self. This is where you start to really learn who you are inside. It is the absolute key to becoming your strongest support system. Building trust and finding safety within is your actual key to survival and making you whole.

Once you learn this independence, you will be forever free of feeling dependent on anyone for anything. It is the worst feeling in the world to have to rely on someone else for something you need to survive or something you need to fill your soul. Once you learn to do this on your own, you find a sense of power, a sense of freedom you could never have imagined. Once you have this, you'll feel safe to start building trust in other people, knowing fully that if they let you down or hurt you in anyway, it will hurt your heart but it will not destroy you. This lesson is complete gold.

"When you focus on you, you grow. When you focus on shit, shit grows."

— Dwayne Johnson

15.

YOUR BODY, YOUR HEALTH

PHYSICAL AND MENTAL WELLNESS

I'm not going to ask you to become a body builder. If you already are one, great work.

A lot of people think of physical wellness as working out and mental wellness as the absence of problems. But, there is so much more to physical wellness than weightlifting, and you will never be problem-free, so this is not true of mental wellness at all either. There are so many areas of wellness we don't even think about.

The actions that we choose to treat our bodies to usually go without thought, but I want to bring to your attention to the importance of changing your thinking. After all, we cannot solve problems by using the same kind of thinking we used when we created them.

The definition of health from the World Health Organization is "a state of complete physical, mental, and social well-being." This should cover everything. It is no longer a reference to the absence of disease. We can do a lot with this holistic approach, and once we acquire wellness in all areas of health, we can start to feel whole.

We're going to start with the basics. For those of you that already have the basics down, consider some of the information in this chapter a review in certain areas, and use it as a reminder for the things you want to improve. As you read through this, I want you to start to develop goals for yourself, and write them down.

WHAT'S IN YOUR KITCHEN

I'm not going to write pages and pages on your meal plans and diet specificities, but I am going to tell you what we have seen from the medical side of fad diets, and why eating whole foods and using portion control are ways your body likes and deserves to be treated.

Let's start with what you decide to put in your mouth and how it is directly impacted by the love you feel for your body. If you are a binge eater, an eater of crap that is not good for you, a strict fad diet user, or an eater that eats to self-soothe, then you are in the same group as pretty much every single other person in the world, at one time in their lives or another. What you feed your body is hands down one of the trickiest tasks most—myself included—struggle with at some point in their lives, if not every day of their lives.

I love food. I honestly love food so much that is it one of the things I look most forward to on certain relaxing evenings or during quick breaks from the busyness of the day. Favourite dates with my husband? Yep, going out for supper and enjoying new foods along with a fine wine and each other's company, away from the kids and the bustle of the everyday. It's during these times that we can release our immediate challenges and deadlines, escape everyone else's demands, and just relax, talk, and eat. It has been said that our emotional attachment to food goes all the way back to our childhoods. It's called comfort food for a reason.

So, think back to your childhood and remember a time when you can relate food to happy feelings. For me, it's ice cream at my grandpa's house. He'd put peanuts on top and stir it for me so that it turned extra soft and creamy and there'd be peanuts with every bite. No matter how hard some days were, I could always count on him making me this dish the same way, every time, and while I sat in the safety of my grandpa and grandma's house full of love for me, I could escape my other life challenges. There I felt so safe and loved. And there it is. Comfort food.

You eat in search of comfort foods as a way to trigger those same safe and happy emotions you once felt as a little girl or boy. You are looking for an excuse to relax for a few minutes, or an opportunity to feel happy and safe because someone you loved used to make you feel loved and cared for when they made you this food, or a way to fill a void you feel in your heart or soul that you don't know how else to fill. It's all emotional.

Maybe you don't like your body so you punish yourself by not eating. Maybe you don't feel worthy of food. Maybe you struggle with eating because you don't actually know what is good for your body and so you just continue habits you have had since you were a child because it's all you know, or because it's easier than trying to change. Either way, at the end of the day, it's all about how you feel and the decisions you choose to make.

I love Ichiban noodles. This is a book of my confessions, apparently. But I do. I love them because every afternoon at two o'clock during the summer when I was off school, my mom and I would take an hour break from whatever tasks we were doing to sit and watch *Another World* together while eating Ichiban noodles. We sat together for an hour, escaping our problems and getting lost in the world of a soap opera show. To this day, whenever I feel I need an hour of escape to be alone with my thoughts, I choose to sit down away from whatever demands are in my life, zone out to a chick flick of some sort, and eat a bowl of steaming Ichiban, all in order to reach those good old feelings of safety and escape. Happiness in a bowl? Seems pathetic when you say it out loud, but I'm trying to be honest about my feelings so you can be honest about yours. So, what do you love eating in order to reach those happy inner child feelings again when you're surrounded by a complex, sometimes painful, adult world?

I love unpacking this kind of stuff. It seems so minor, but it is seriously important in the world of why. Almost all of the conscious things we do or choices we make have subconscious drivers behind the scenes. The reason I am even bringing this up is to get you to understand your subconscious drivers so that you can change your behaviours if those behaviours are causing you problems with your physical or mental health today.

Today, I don't crave ice cream or Ichiban very often, but sometimes triggering those old emotions is just what I need. So, what should we do about it? Should we forbid ourselves to eat that chocolate or those chips or whatever it is you love? Depends who you listen to! Everyone has a different opinion on this topic, and every one of those people are sure they are right. Be a vegan! Be a vegetarian! Don't eat carbs! Do keto and get all that fat in! Stay away from fatty foods! Only eat the good fatty foods! Eat mostly meat! Eat only organic! Fasting is the only way! Steamed chicken and broccoli every day! Seriously, this is bound to confuse anyone trying to actually find out how to improve your health. Too much information in opposing directions makes for some serious overwhelm, which can leave you feeling defeated and still unknowing. So, I am going to simplify things for you, because the world needs to be a little simpler.

First thing's first: do not do fad diets. Improve your energy, lose body fat—that's always the goal with any general diet plan, isn't it? I want to be clear that one of my biggest pet peeves in the world of dieting is fad diets. I hate them so much. I also hate strict rules that nobody can actually live by for long periods of time. I hate empty promises and fake ads about taking weight loss pills, doing nothing else, and still losing weight. The easy way out never works! This is true in any area of your life. Habitual changes take hard work. They are the compound effect of continued actions, commitment, and the mental capacity and motivation to sacrifice unhealthy shortcuts to feeling good now in favour of your healthier future self.

On the surgical unit I worked on, we saw so many cases of cholecystitis (inflammation of the gallbladder) from people on the keto diet. The job of your gallbladder is to store bile for the breakdown and digestion of fats once they are released into your small intestine. People who are on keto for a long time have so much fat built up in their bodies that it causes a major back up in the function of your gallbladder. Your cholesterol will also skyrocket if you are on keto for a long period of time (over three months).

People love keto because when they stick to it, it works for losing weight. I am not against a head start if you want to make a drastic change in a couple of weeks or even a month, but for some that continue for a long period of time, their bodies can become confused and end up undergoing upset body systems, possibly requiring hospitalization and removal of their gallbladders.

The point of this example is not "don't do keto." I don't care what you end up deciding to do, as this whole book and my whole philosophy is about autonomy and the ability to decide what is best for yourself. But what I want you to have is real-life information that you wouldn't find in a podcast or book that tells you to do keto. As I said earlier, information about diets can get very confusing. So, I am here to put on my nurse hat strictly to give you information about how your body physically and emotionally works around food.

The thing you need to know about all these diets like the cabbage soup diet, Atkins, metabolism pills, fasting for long periods of time, and so on for the hundreds of others out there, is that once you stop it, you will gain the weight back. On top of that, every diet you try will affect your hormone balance and blood sugars and confuse your metabolism. This has a direct correlation with your emotional health. Have you ever been "hangry"? You *know* it's a real thing. People get very cranky when they are hungry. So, let's just focus more on changing old habits and not choosing instant pleasure to Band-Aid deeper problems.

Now that we've established that fad diets are not worth the hype, we can return to the principle of keeping it simple. Focus on wholesome foods and portion control. My metabolism used to be pretty good, so I never used to worry about calorie counting, or being conscious of what I eat. Enter my late twenties and my body started changing and reacting to food in a way I wasn't used to. Over were my days of eating whatever I wanted, whenever I wanted. But, once I realized that in most cases I was eating more out of an emotional requirement rather than actually being hungry, it helped me with portion control. If you have ever been really hungry, you will eat carrots, apples, broccoli, whatever is closest. If you are snacking and you don't want carrots or broccoli, most likely you are not as hungry as you think you are. Drink some water instead. Sometimes we are dehydrated without even knowing it, and so we search for food in order to try and pull water from it.

Calorie counting is a perfect way to start learning how many calories are actually in the foods you consume. When I first started counting calories, I was shocked at how much I was actually eating. You can find more information, including formulas, on how to determine how many calories you should be consuming in books like Michael Matthews's *Thinner Leaner Stronger*. The important thing is to find a book with guidance that connects to your belief system and with what you are willing to do and not do. Many people think they know it all on this topic, so be particular in who you seek information from and keep it simple for yourself. Remember that weight loss equals calories in less than calories burned. Once you start staying within the allotted calorie count you have set out for yourself, it will give you an idea of how much your body actually needs for its basal metabolic rate (the amount of calories required to keep all of your organs working so that you stay alive) and then how much you need in order to replace any extra activity you are performing. Remember to research maintenance after weight loss, and add exercise to your life for the sake of your body's physical movement and muscle strength. Remember that 75% of your plate should be comprised of protein, vegetables, fruits, and dairy.

One thing I'll say though, is that calorie counting can be a restrictive mindset for some, so it is not ideal for anyone with a history of or susceptibility to disordered eating, as calorie counting can be triggering for those affected. This method needs to be executed responsibly, with health and wellness as your main priority. It's important to think of it more as permission to eat within your allotted count. You can eat what you want, keeping in mind foods that lack nutrients will add to your calorie count for the day, without providing health benefits to your body. The goal with eating more wholesome foods and limiting processed foods is to increase your nutritional intake with essential vitamins and minerals to keep your body systems working at an optimal level. This will give you more energy and improve your mood. Eating crap might feel good in the moment thanks to an initial release of feel-good hormones, but the emotions you might have afterward can plunge you into shame and the huge digestion project you just gave your internal system to process will result in decreased energy. If you repeat this cycle, you will find yourself lacking certain nutrients and vitamins you need to sustain optimal health for each of your body systems. Consider increasing your protein intake to balance blood sugar and muscle growth or maintenance. Eat fruits and vegetable to acquire vitamins and minerals such as vitamin A, C, E, magnesium, zinc, phosphorous, folic acid, and fibre. They contain natural sugar and are low in fats.

Once you actually start doing something you have set your mind to, you will start to feel pride when you see results. You will feel more energy the healthier you eat. Weight loss absolutely comes 80% from the kitchen with portion control (calorie counting). More specifically, healthy eating involves decreasing intake of processed foods, late night snacking, overeating until you feel overly full or immediately tired after eating, and not eating if your body is not actually hungry. Keep it simple.

Finally, keep in mind that eating around a restrictive mindset never works in the long term. If you restrict yourself from indulging in your most-loved foods, you will not succeed. End of story. Just be mindful of when and how often you choose to indulge. Remember that food is meant to be a loving addition to our bodies. I mean, it actually keeps us alive, so that makes sense. Most of us have developed an unhealthy relationship with food along the way through our lives, but once we understand why we feel certain ways about eating, we can better understand how to change those habits that are not serving us.

EMOTIONAL EATING

Back to the correlation between food and our emotions. The relationships we hold with food are very complex. In most cases, they can be taken back to our experiences in childhood, and they have absolutely everything to do with self-worth. Many people suffer from eating disorders, and at the core of each of those people is a hurt little child that lives inside of them.

Trauma, judgment from others, abuse in any form, comparing to others in search of self-worth, and filling a void or empty feeling in our hearts are the causes of most unhealthy relationships with food. Once we develop respect for ourselves, we begin to feed our bodies healthy foods as a way of providing love and support for them, rather than damaging them due to a lack of care for our own wellbeing. When you love yourself, you want to take care of yourself.

For those of you in a stage of self-destruction, this book should be your wake-up call. I would gladly hear your story and be your support system as you find your self-worth again, because my heart aches for anyone that is not being nice to themselves. Hear my words when I tell you that it is not up to anyone else to decide how valuable you are. You have no idea how important and worthy you are.

Seek professional help if you are the victim of an eating disorder, or if you are eating to fill the void left by a lack of love or the loss of a loved one. Therapy is a natural way of validating and releasing those emotions that are inside of you.

Talking to yourself can be very beneficial as well. When you eat something, ask, why did I want to eat this right now? What emotions do I feel as I eat it? What do those emotions remind me of? When did I last feel those emotions? Maybe this food is something you used to eat in your childhood that caused positive emotions or feelings of love and safety, and eating that comfort food today helps you to fill whatever void you are trying to fill, like me when I eat ice cream or Ichiban. Maybe that void is hurt, maybe it's loneliness? Whatever it is, start to reflect on it. Start to name the emotions, allow yourself to drift off in thought, and see what your innate guidance tells you or what memories start to show up. Once you start to unpack things, you will find progress in understanding yourself on a deeper level. There's always a why to things. But, in the case where eating a certain unhealthy food just seems to be a habit that brings pleasure? Find a new healthy habit that brings pleasure to replace the old habit, and keep practising that instead.

How you look at yourself in the mirror affects how you feel about yourself entirely. Start the practice of accepting your body first and foremost just as you are today. Stop that inner critical self when she or he starts talking down to you, remove yourself from anyone that talks down to you or criticizes you in any way. Start each day by finding the things you like about yourself and say them out loud in the mirror. It sounds so silly! But please try it, it will get easier to hear the good things the more you practice saying them. As for the things you wish to change or improve, make this your goal and start right away in developing a plan to achieve this goal. If you start to listen to yourself and not let yourself down, you will start to feel less shame and more pride. Things like going for a run, lifting weights, joining a class or a new sport, eating healthy, and practicing healthy self-talk will help to develop pride if done as promised to yourself. If you slip up, skip a day, give yourself grace and keep trying. Once you achieve the thing you set out to do, everything starts to change. Momentum starts to build and more and more positive things begin to unfold.

HYDRATE ME.

Water helps to clear your body of toxins and unwanted bacteria; aids in digestion by pulling water from your circulatory system into your bowels to help move stool and waste; increases the health of your bowels; helps to normalize blood pressure; supports joint, organ, and tissue health; helps to regulate body temperature; maintains electrolyte balance; and helps with tissue cell maintenance and growth by carrying nutrients and oxygen through the hydrated blood supply.

How much water to drink depends on many factors, such as your body weight, your level of activity, the temperature of your living environment, and what medications you are taking. You can calculate your custom weight-to-water ratio, or you can just keep it simple and ensure that you drink eight to twelve cups of water per day.

Most times when we think we are hungry, our bodies may just need more water. So, we should drink one to two cups of water, wait fifteen minutes, and then see if we still feel hungry.

Decreasing alcohol intake is also very beneficial to your body's health and wellness, as alcohol affects every body system eventually. Quite like the way that smoking damages your lungs, we do not see the compound effect that drinking alcohol and eating unhealthy foods has on our organs until it starts to affect our body systems, and by that time the damage has already been done.

Hopefully these little tips and tricks will help in guiding you or reminding you that if we are good to our bodies, we will feel the effects of it. Developing self-worth goes hand-in-hand with wanting to be kind to our bodies, wanting to feel our best, and wanting to increase the longevity of our lives. Respect your body as it's the only one you will have in this life. Once it begins to fail, you cannot reverse time. Your health greatly affects the quality of life you have, so making your physical and mental health a priority will change every aspect of your life.

WELL, WE ALL KNOW THIS ONE

Exercising your body is at the core of health and wellness—both physical and mental. It is absolutely necessary. If you want to improve your cardiovascular health and physical stamina, start training in running or take on lane swimming, bike riding, a group sport, or fitness classes—whatever gives you pleasure while getting your heart rate up. If you want to increase your strength, start lifting weights at home or join a gym, do yoga, or do body weight strength building. Pick a routine you are comfortable with and actually follow through with it. Throughout it all, always keep measurable goals.

Exercise contributes to two very important things: physical health and mental health. The physical aspects are endless. Muscle strength gives us the ability to endure life's physical requirements so that we can complete our day-to-days, as well as endure other physical work, like caring for others. It also allows us to feel good about the way we look in our bodies. When we commit to regular strength training, we are making promises to ourselves, and as we start to see results, we also start to feel pride. This is how we build trust in ourselves, and it is where self-confidence really starts.

Improved cardiovascular health also comes with exercise. It includes a strengthened and better-maintained heart muscle which, as you know, pumps blood throughout your entire body. This is so important to every body system and each internal organ as the body systems are all connected, and every part of our body needs blood flow to provide it with nutrients. Do you want healthier skin and hair? Get that blood pumping through to bring your skin cells more oxygen and nutrients from your vascular supply. Eating healthily and taking vitamins feeds our bodies the nutrients we need, our digestive systems break these nutrients down, and our hearts actually pump the nutrients throughout our bodies, so cardiovascular health is so very important.

The other key aspect to cardiovascular health is the prevention of heart attack and stroke. Your heart is a muscle and when you exercise you are strengthening that muscle, allowing for an increase in the efficiency in which your heart pumps blood throughout your body. The stronger and more efficient your heart can pump decreases the rate it has to work to move the blood to all your organs. Oxygen consumption will be higher, your blood pressure and heart rate will be lower. Think of it like tuning up your engine. The engine here is your heart and circulatory system, and it will be working more efficiently preventing plaque from building up in your blood vessels that cause heart attacks and strokes. You may be young and vital now, but you won't always have youth on your side. Your older self will be very grateful to your younger self and for the health of your organs if you take care of them now.

Now, on to mental health. On top of all the physical aspects we gain from exercise, there are many mental and emotional benefits as well. Any type of movement provides an outlet for stress and emotion, while also increasing the release of serotonin and norepinephrine, which are mood-enhancing hormones. They help us feel happier, and they help decrease anxiety and depression. Exercise also increases our dopamine levels, a neurotransmitter that plays a role in body functions such as movement, memory, motivation, and pleasurable reward. It helps us feel better.

The other very simple but super important aspect of mental health that is related to exercise is the energy flow that happens when we do it. This aspect is on more of a spiritual level, so if you can open your mind to it, it will greatly improve your mental clarity and feelings of contentment. When we talk about energy flow in the spirit world, it can be easier to understand and believe if we take it back to grade school science class when we learned about atoms and cells. In biology, energy provides the ability to do work— in order for a cell to function, it requires energy. You may remember that energy is never lost, but it can be converted from one form to another. Kinetic energy, potential energy, chemical energy, thermal energy... the point of this trip down biology class memory lane is that we are all made of energy. So, energy exists, and toxic energy from unresolved emotions or past trauma is detrimental to our health. We have energy chakras within our bodies that can get blocked, preventing the flow of energy through our body systems. Anxiety is a by-product of stagnant toxic energy stuck in our bodies, so in order to remove it, we must exercise.

When we move our bodies, we move the energy within us on so many levels, right down to the work of each cell in each body system, including our brains. So, moving our bodies equals feeling better. Under all of that brilliant science, it really is that simple.

DON'T LET THIS SHOCK YOU

Now for a little word on the topic that affects your health and wellness just as much as breathing, eating, and drinking water.

Healthy sleep is imperative for cognitive function, mood regulation, cardiovascular, and metabolic health. Those of you that lack sleep some days can attest to this, as it can leave you with a foggy brain, cranky mood, and hungover type of feeling, even without having had any alcohol. Our body systems and our brains work most efficiently when we are rested. For those of you with babies or young kids, seriously approaching deadlines, or sick family members—your lack of sleep is a season, and you can do what you have to do at the time. But for general health and wellness with optimal mood enhancement, sex drive, digestion, and performance of basic bodily functions, you need proper sleep.

The National sleep foundation suggests obtaining on average seven to nine hours per night for adults for optimal health, teenagers require eight to ten hours, school aged children should sleep nine to twelve hours, young children ages one to five require ten to fourteen hours, and infants twelve months and under require twelve to sixteen hours. It is when we are asleep that our body repairs itself; cells resupply energy storage, heal injuries, and repair tissues. Our brain works through sorted memories, and processes learned information increasing the efficiency of access and use of the new knowledge. From a cellular level, this rest required in healing and repair in our organs, tissues, and brain function makes it imperative that we prioritize sleep when we are able. Unless you have kids, in which case you are screwed. Haha.

"You're imperfect, and you're wired for struggle, but you are worthy of love and belonging."

— Brené Brown

16.

I THINK WE SHOULD TALK

I hate small talk. I really hate it. It's like, "So, the weather sure is nice today. I like your sweater." "Thanks. Yes, it sure is nice out." Wow. Let's save ourselves from spending time on this meaningless chit-chat. How about another one: "How are you today?" Most people answer with, "Good, and you?" even though their tired, glossy eyes tell you that they may not be answering truthfully. People answer this way for two reasons:

1. *They don't want to tell a stranger* their life story or about the heaviness that is sitting in their hearts.

2. *They don't want anyone to know* about their heavy hearts. People want other people to think everything is fine. They don't want to show any vulnerabilities.

Well, guess what? This needs to stop. Immediately. It has become too easy to hide behind social media posts and to tell ourselves that we are not lonely. We need to get back to actually talking to each other.

You know when one of your friends calls you rather than texts you, and you immediately think, *I hope everything is OK*? What the hell happened there? Why is calling to talk considered so out of the norm now? What are we teaching our young people? The world has become connected in so many ways with social media, but the utter fact of this is that it has created a new lack of vulnerability in conversation and has made for a fake life around us.

Confidence comes from not feeling alone and not feeling inferior to those that are faking it. When you look more closely at people and have the opportunity to dig a little deeper into their truthful thoughts, you learn that we are not all that different from each other. And we absolutely are not all as confident as we may seem. Even the ones you thought were so damn beautiful and smart. When you really talk to them, you will very quickly learn that they have many vulnerabilities and many things they don't like about themselves too. Why? Because someone has hurt them at some point in their lives too. Someone has thrown them a comment that sits deep inside of them, someone has mistreated them, or someone has just been mean to them. Most likely because of envy, sometimes because of abuse. Either way, you cannot un-hear someone's words, and it is a whole lot easier to believe the bad stuff.

I want to talk about sex.

I THINK WE SHOULD TALK

What does sex have to do with small talk? Nothing. But it has everything to do with confidence which is what I really want to talk to you about. When you give yourself to someone, you are at your most vulnerable. It is so personal, private, sacred, raw... all the words. It can be completely amazing—or completely devastating. Some of you may have made choices around sex that you regret today. Maybe you made a lot of choices you regret. Those choices have everything to do with self-worth. I want you to look at your choices from a non-judgmental standpoint. Hear me out before you tell me you can't do that because you very much do judge yourself for those choices—I want you to just step outside of that for a minute, and look at yourself from a different perspective. I want you to look at yourself through the eyes of someone that loves you.

Think of little you. You are young, innocent, learning about the world around you. Then someone hurts you. Maybe it's a physical hurt, maybe it's sexual, maybe it's verbal. But it really hurts. Think back to this and remember everything you can about it. Let the tears fall if they start, but don't worry if they don't. I just want you to remember how you felt in that moment. Your heart will start to feel like something is squeezing it, or like it is sinking in your chest. You will start to feel a knot in your stomach or a lump in your throat. If little you were instead your own daughter, sister, friend, mother, son, brother, or even a random little girl or boy, you would feel sorry for them for hurting. So, when you look at your younger self through these same, unconditionally loving eyes, you should feel sorry for yourself. You should feel empathy for that little person and you should begin to understand where they were when they started making unhealthy choices.

It is so important to understand that we are not born wanting to do destructive things. We are products of our environments, and the choices we make do not always reflect who we really are inside. In most cases, when we make choices we regret, we aren't thinking much about them at the time. We are just reacting to the moment we are in and using the knowledge and life experience we've accumulated up until that point to make those choices. But multiply this by a lot more moments and we end up somewhere wondering how the hell we actually got there. Only looking back now that we are outside of the situation and the emotions that accompanied it are the decisions easier to follow and judge.

So, what does this have to do with sex? Again, it has everything to do with it, and self-worth is at the very centre of it all. Sex is part of a healthier you, if you can find a way for it to meet your emotional needs and your sexual needs from a confident place. It is when our self-worth is low and when we are unsure of who we really are inside that we make choices about sex that we may not be happy with later in our lives.

I'm going to tell you a story of my own about self-worth, guidance, choices, being single, and a guy I met one night. Only this night actually changed my life. It changed me because at that time, I was one of those broken souls going down a dangerous path based on my past, which I had no idea was affecting me in the way that our pasts tend to do. It was a time in my life when all I knew how to do was to act on my emotions. I had not yet learned about reflecting and reasoning before acting or about unpacking trauma or past experiences and relating them to the person we become. If I can teach you a few things about self-worth and creating a better life, it will hopefully save you from going through the pain of learning these lessons through your own life experiences, or maybe it will equip you to recognize it in your child when you find them in that season of teenager life. This story is about how easy it is for a girl to reach out to the arms of a man in hopes of filling a void in her heart—a story that I think repeats itself in many girls these days.

I had just moved to Calgary. I was twenty years old and had decided to move in with a friend I had met in college. She was so much fun and so beautiful, and the thing I loved the most about her was that she had a normal life. She had a nice mom and dad and she'd grown up in a nice house in a community with normal people that worked and raised their families. That's what she'd told me anyway. It was so fresh to me! She also came from a family that had money, so none of them had made any awful choices due to financial stress. Living with her felt like I finally had a chance to escape the darkness and constant challenges I had in my life with my family. I had just settled my mom in with my aunt and uncle after being on the run for a few months, hiding her from my angry father. We had been living on the road, staying with other friends I had met in college so that my dad would have no way to connect with us. That way, we were able to stay safe long enough to talk everything through and come up with a plan to change our way of living. Once I knew my mom was safe, I left for Calgary to find my exciting, new, safe, normal place. And that's where I met him. The tall, dark, and handsome guy that changed everything.

After I told my beautiful friend about my story, she poured us a few drinks and told me I needed to go out and let off some steam. She lived her life working, partying, and living a single life that included a lot of male company coming into and out of her dating life, as well as her bedroom. She loved this life. So footloose and carefree. It was crazy to me! She had no dark stories holding her captive. She was just young and fun, dancing, drinking, meeting guys, having sex, relaxing, living in the cute little condo her parents had bought for her, and enjoying her life.

I thought about this as I accepted the drink from her. Hmmm. Maybe I did need to be more like her so that I could have what she had. Her life was so easy and fun. I wanted that for my life! So, off I went. After feeding me some shots, we got all dressed up and headed downtown to a bar called Coyotes. Everything felt scary and exciting all at once. When we walked in, it was like I was all of sudden living in someone else's life. The lights were dim, music was pumping, people were everywhere. This bar was bigger than any I had ever seen, and to be honest, it felt a bit like I was in a movie. I was that character from a small town, the naïve little farm girl out in the big bad city—the land of opportunity, of new beginnings, and of new boys to shake things up.

All of my problems in real life just faded away. Even if it was just for the night, it felt so good. I felt so free. My friend and I walked toward the bar to order drinks, and that's when I saw him. Tall, dark, and handsome. Just like in the movies, our eyes met. I could read his mind when he looked at me... I smiled at him and kept walking to the bar.

That night, my friend and I drank and danced with so many guys. I hadn't had that much fun in a long time. I saw the same boy watching me throughout the night, but we never talked. He just made eye contact with me every once in a while when I looked his way.

Toward the end of the night, I started feeling my burdens surfacing again. I had had fun, but the drinks were wearing off and my heart started hurting again. The weight was back. The one where my shoulders and chest felt heavy and I couldn't take a calm deep breath. It was a swirling storm, circling, moving through my soul. I hated that my escape had felt so short. Things started flashing through me: thoughts of things my dad had said and done to me, a vision of my mom's face full of fear and hurt, the pain of missing my little brother. All of a sudden, I was pulled out of my escape by a blast of reality, and I knew that all of this would be waiting for me when I woke up the next

I THINK WE SHOULD TALK

morning. I didn't want to go back to feeling it. I wanted to stay in my escape. And I wanted to feel loved. Cherished. I wanted to be held.

So, I walked up to him. I looked up at his handsome face, and his eyes lit up. I couldn't help but smile. He seemed so laid back, calm, and stoic. He set his beer down and we left to go back to my friend's condo.

Looking back now, my thirty-nine-year-old self cannot believe I did that. I invited a complete stranger back to our condo. Remember that movie I had felt like I was in earlier, with the naïve, young, small-town farm girl? Yeah, that could easily have turned into a horror movie where the young farm girl and her friend didn't make it out alive. The little pig farmer that went on a date and got murdered. Oh, my Lord. The things young people do when they think they are invincible... or when they don't really care if something bad does happen to them.

Anyway. He didn't kill me. And my girlfriend said she brought people home with her all the time, so I guess I thought it was the "normal" thing to do. You know, when you were twenty, you didn't have to hide your mom from your mean dad, deal with both of their drinking every day, or deal with the pain of losing your little brother and the destruction it brought to the rest of your family... you just met a boy at a bar and hung out with that boy. That second choice seemed like a much better option. Plus, I really liked how he made me feel when he looked at me. Like he had been waiting to meet someone like me. Maybe he liked the way I looked, or maybe his soul knew that my soul was broken and secretly wanted a strong, tall, handsome man to fix it all and fill my lonely, hurting heart. Yes. The classic thing a person with low self-worth seeks when they don't know any better: someone to come to their rescue.

We stayed up all night sitting cross-legged across from each other on the floor, talking and laughing, flirting and sipping on whisky. He definitely took me away from reality. And then he kissed me. I had never felt so wanted, so special, so beautiful. The adventure of it all, the way he made me feel... And that's how choices are made—by riding those emotions. Reacting and not really knowing. Sound familiar to anyone? If so, you can guess how the story ended that night then. It was most definitely passionate, and I did feel cherished for at least a few short hours.

A quick fix that didn't really fix anything that my soul really needed in the long term. My heart remained empty and my problems still awaited me. I kept up a relationship with him for a couple of months afterward, hoping I could find something in him that I was missing in me.

Now, the crazy thing about life is that there are these pivotal moments where your life changes, just like that. This turned out to be one of them.

They say that girls look for a man that has the qualities of her father. Well, I seemed to fit that pattern. The guys I had dated up to that point had all had one thing in common: they all treated me like shit. This guy though, he seemed different in the beginning. He seemed like he honestly cherished me. But, time passed by, and he got a little more comfortable. He started saying things that were very controlling. He started becoming demanding, making it clear that I had better answer his calls when they came in and make myself available for him when he wanted me to be. These were all red flags for me, and my soul recognized them, but I let them go on longer than I should have, just in case I was maybe being too sensitive. Self-doubt is easy when you don't really have a clear example of what it is to be treated properly. It makes things very confusing for a young girl. Unfortunately, most young girls have to learn these lessons the hard way before they can really understand and appreciate how they deserve to be treated.

Just like any lesson in life, to find out what you like, you must first find out what you don't like. The message became clear to me one night while we were being intimate. He suddenly became forceful and rough. When I looked into his eyes, I recognized the look immediately. My soul knew. It was like I could read his mind; his eyes were a window into his toxic, troubled soul. I obeyed him that night for fear of what I knew would most likely happen to me if I didn't. As I laid there after it was over, I made a promise to myself that I would no longer see him again and that I would not follow in my mother's footsteps.

The message from my soul was clear, and I listened. I no longer felt cherished by him. I felt controlled and worthless. I wanted absolutely nothing to do with him or the hurt he would one day cause me, and I wanted nothing to do with any other man moving forward. The best chance I had to keep myself safe was to stay single and on my own forever if I had to. I found my independence that day. That was the first life-changing lesson in my story.

So, to all of the broken girls out there: your gut feelings, your intuition, the feeling you get in your chest and your lungs and your throat, the knot you feel in your stomach, the voice you hear inside your body like it is talking to your head—this is your guidance. I call it God. Whatever it is to you, you need to quiet down your thoughts and listen to it. Just like they taught us when we were small and crossing the road: stop, look, and listen. Listen to your gut feelings and intuition when you are looking for someone to love.

The process of developing self-worth and independence is so important to self-care and physical and mental health. Knowing just how valuable and precious you are is the first step in developing independence. Know that only you get to decide what you do with your body. This is the very first and most important thing to understand about self-worth. You are the boss of yourself and your body. Nobody else gets to decide what you do. Once you begin to understand this, you can begin to make wiser choices regarding what is best for your soul and for your present and future self. And once you gain trust in yourself and the choices you make, you begin to really understand that the one and only person you truly need is you. From there, the rest will follow to complete your heart.

All aspects of holistic health are intertwined. Your sexual health must be a focus that is just as important as eating healthily and exercising. I wanted to write a chapter about sex because I think it gets forgotten about a lot in our busy lives when it is absolutely something that should not be forgotten about. A lot of us are taught young that sex is shameful, sex is bad, sex is something we don't talk about. If you have ever been sexually abused, it creates a whole world of problems when you try to find enjoyment in this area again. It takes a lot of crying and working through things for those of you that have suffered physical or verbal hurt to your bodies. These are things that we need to prioritize fixing in all of us, and especially in the broken ones among us.

What we are not taught in most cases is just how sacred sex is. When you enter or when someone enters your body, you are literally allowing them to enter your soul. But when you are young, troubled, and haven't been taught about this part of self-worth, you view sex more as a task to please. This is not OK, and it needs to change. I am here to remind you that sex is not something to be taken lightly, and when you agree to partake in it with someone, you need to be fully present while you do so.

For all of you people pleasers out there, sex is about you too. It is not just an act to please someone else or meet someone else's needs. For most of my life, I also focused on trying to please in this area, and I put my own needs right off the map. I wasn't concerned with meeting my own needs because if I could meet the needs of the person I was being intimate with, then maybe they would fall in love with me. I was your typical young girl with no self-worth mentality. If this is you, I want this to change for you. It wasn't until a few years into my married life that I started to focus on my own needs in the bedroom, and now that I have found my self-worth, I love sex in a way I never knew I could before. It's important, so don't dismiss it anymore.

Take the time to self-reflect on your past experiences, read books, or seek professional help if you need in order to feel more comfortable as you unpack the toxic crap that might live inside of you. Learn to love your body, and learn to be very specific about else who gets to love your body too.

Sexual and emotional satisfaction looks different for those in relationships compared to those who are single, but the basis of how sex makes us feel is the same no matter our relationship status. We all want to be loved, we all want to feel desired, and we all want to feel safe. When you are single, it can be hard to balance meeting your sexual needs with finding and developing a relationship with someone that makes you feel loved and safe. Some just want a sexual release with no emotional attachment so that they don't have to let their guards down for fear of getting hurt, losing someone they fall in love with, or dealing with rejection. For these folks, just having sex is just easier. This Band-Aid may work for a while, but deep down, everyone wants to be loved, so these actions can eventually cause deeper heartache and leave your soul feeling unfulfilled.

For those in relationships, sex can become just as complicated if it is not cared for from a healthy standpoint. There are times in a relationship when it may feel like a chore to meet the needs of your partner, especially when you are already trying to meet the needs of so many other people in your day-to-day. Your kids may need you, or you may face work demands. This leaves limited time for self-care, and when the house finally gets quiet and you get a chance to rest or lay your head down... there he is, moving closer to you and looking at you with that look. You know the one. Well, this is every person in a relationship at some point in their lives. Meeting one another's sexual needs is so important, but here you are, exhausted! Every relationship goes through stages and every person goes through seasons, so this will repeatedly be a challenge that each of us faces, whether we are single or attached. One of the most important things you can do to keep a healthy relationship around meeting each other's needs is open communication and a willingness to balance both your needs and your partners. Respect for each other and how you each are feeling in your experiences makes for a strong brick layer in your relationship. Some seasons are harder than others. Respecting one another and focusing on open and clear communication makes it easier to trudge through those harder days.

Meeting the needs of the person we are with is a huge part of a healthy relationship, but it needs to be done with the consideration of both parties. It is normal in the season of building a family with demanding children and limited time to rest for you to feel too tired and busy to dedicate time to connecting in the bedroom. The thing about this though is that when sexual intimacy is put on the back burner, time can pass by quite quickly. If someone in the relationship has unmet needs because of this, it can sometimes lead to them looking elsewhere to meet those needs they crave. This can be sex or emotional attachment when the need for romantic attention or the feeling of being cherished isn't being met at home. This is a danger zone for couples. Life can change very quickly for those in this zone. When you choose someone to spend your life with, you choose to do so with the person you know today. But, if there's one thing in life that you can count on, it's that people change.

As couples grow, some begin to grow apart. If you choose to have kids with someone, the two of you must come first in order to give your family a chance to stay whole. It has always been said that the kids come first, but given how easy it is to fall out of love with someone and want out these days, it is imperative we change how we view our priorities. If you are currently in a relationship that is healthy, you will want to work hard in keeping your passion alive. It seems almost impossible to do during the busy seasons of raising babies, chasing careers, or sometimes doing both at the same time. But believe you me, you will not regret changing a few priorities once in a while to set aside time to communicate with and make love to your partner. If it means you get to feel fulfilled in your relationship and your family gets to stay whole, it is worth it. For those of you that are not sure if you want to be with your partner anymore, it means that a lot of needs from both parties are not being met, and it is up to the two of you to decide if meeting these needs is something you are both willing to work on—if your relationship, at this point, is worth saving.

Some of you have a healthy sex drive and quite enjoy being intimate with your partner. Others of you might feel depleted and resentful in having to meet your partner's needs on top of everything else you have to do. It may feel like all you do is look after everyone else's needs and sex may be the last thing on your mind.

We are innately born with a desire to be intimate, and we are innately born with feelings of sexual desire. It is the whole reason we are able to procreate. Women's sexual desire cycles on a thirty-day pattern along with the moon, and men are on a twenty-four-hour cycle. This makes for very different experiences for both parties. The hormones involved in a woman's cycle play a massive role in her sex drive. If our hormones are out of balance (which 95% of women's are) we can struggle with sex drive, conceiving, mood swings, low energy levels, and anxiety and depression. Hormone production is a part of a body system in itself, and it affects every other body system as they are all intertwined. Menstruation, birth control, and pregnancy throws the cycle right off balance, and for some it can be very hard to get it back on track. Lack of sleep, lack of rest, poor diet, and lack of exercise also have everything to do with hormone balance.

There should be a time in your cycle when you feel introverted, crave rest, and need time to reflect. With most women, this is usually at the time of the new moon, though for some it can be the opposite and fall on the full moon. Some women cycle opposite each other to provide a balance for those in the rest stage. There should be a time in your cycle when you feel energized, vibrant, more confident, extroverted, and higher in energy. This is the time around ovulation, and it is at this time that you should naturally feel a higher sex drive. All revved up. This is during the full moon for most, but for those opposite, they will feel this on the new moon.

When you ovulate, you give off pheromones. First studied in ancient Greece, pheromones are hormones secreted to induce activity in other individuals... sexual arousal. Think about this: have you ever had a time when you were out and about and you attracted more people than usual into conversation or flirting? When you felt more confident and energized than usual? And, be honest here, you felt a little more sexually aroused than usual? Looking around at perky butts or bulging muscles? Don't pretend you don't know what I mean because I know it has happened to you. This is the natural cycle I am referring to—it is literally how we were designed to make babies. God created us to reproduce, and like my energetic little pug that goes around humping my kid's stuffed animals, we are also animalistic in our sex needs.

So, knowing that this is a normal part of our cycles, if you haven't felt this way for a while, you can now recognize that this could possibly be because of a hormone imbalance or a lack of sleep and self-care! What you need to do after you have recognized the problem is to seek knowledge on how to fix it. Read books, see your medical health practitioner, try a naturopath, research online, or listen to podcasts related to the subject. There is so much information out there about low sex drive, but make sure you are reading or listening to professionals about it. Many people without the appropriate background knowledge have offered their opinions, and they're all different, so it can leave you feeling very confused on your path to finding a solution. For reference, here's what I do to keep myself sexually healthy:

> *I follow the moon's cycle* to help remind myself of where I am in my own cycle. It reminds me to think, like, *Oh yeah, this is my time to reflect, which is why I don't feel like being around people as much right now or why I feel extra tired or irritable.* Or, *This is my time to initiate and tackle my goals because my energy is high and I feel like being around people and being involved.* If anything, tracking the moon helps provide me with grace when I'm wondering why I'm so introverted some days. Reflection time is food for our souls—that's why it's built into our cycles.

- *I take time to listen* to how my body is feeling as well as what my moods and energy levels are. I pay attention to my tolerance of things that irritate me, and I reflect on if it is off base from what my usual natural reaction is. This helps me decipher if the issue is more to do with the other person or if I am being extra sensitive at the time.

- *I do whatever I can* to try and rest when I feel I need to. I was never good at this, but for the last couple of years, I have made a good effort to prioritize self-care, reward myself for hard work, and rest when I need to. Even so, I still struggle with slowing down. It really takes a lot of practise for all of us movers and shakers out there. If you are familiar with the Enneagram personality system, it is the achiever in me. But adequate rest really changes overall health and wellness in an incredible way.

- *I prioritize making healthy choices* in the kitchen to truly feel the benefits of eating whole foods and decreasing the crap that goes into my body. If you have made this a priority as well, then you know exactly what benefits I am talking about. My body feels cleaner and more regulated, my energy level is higher, I feel more confident in my body, my sex drive is increased, and I feel happier. Choosing healthier eating choices takes dedication and practise, and I have given myself the go-ahead to indulge in the foods I love during certain times because I simply love food so much and don't want to completely give up the ability to treat myself.

- *I exercise.* Running is my passion, but lifting weights feels great too. I have trouble with wanting to lift, but the aftereffects of the work are definitely worth it. My body also loves when I do yoga, as it feels great to be stretched and to build muscle strength. Shavasana at the end is the best rest and meditation. But, setting aside the quiet time for yoga is hard for me, especially when I just really crave going outside and running in the fresh air. I am lucky that running is something I crave doing, so cardio is mostly my go-to exercise. It's where I leave my stress and problems—behind me on the path. I literally feel them being released from me on my run. My thoughts go through a processing system and the negative energy disintegrates into the open air. My favourite routine is cardio or weights and then yoga to follow. This all takes time to do though, so when my time and energy are limited, I just pick one activity and do it.

- *I meditate!* This is so important. Seriously. Read books about it, practise it, do it every day. This is the best rest for your brain and your body, and you will take so much from it. This is also where solutions arise and reflections get sorted. It is my favourite thing to do.

- *I take a lot of vitamins.* After you hit adrenal burnout, it takes a lot to refuel and rebuild your stamina. I find that feeding my adrenal health by supplementing minerals and vitamins that my food may not have enough of or that I may not be eating enough of helps me to feel balanced and complete.

Doing these things seems to be working for me, but everyone is different. Develop your own unique plan specific to your body and lifestyle needs.

> *"Before you act, listen. Before you react, think. Before you spend, earn. Before you criticize, wait. Before you pray, forgive. Before you quit, try."*
> — Ernest Hemingway

17.

GET RICH

When most people think of wealth, they think of money. Well, money is definitely a part of wealth, but what most don't realize is that there are many areas of your life that can make you wealthy. Have you ever noticed that some people are more successful in certain areas of their lives than others? Some have such supportive relationships and seem to have a lot of people they are close with in their lives, while others have a lot money, successful careers, or extreme physical fitness. And some seem to have it all.

When I started on my healing journey, I began to learn about the different parts of life that we can be successful in and how each one ties into our physical and mental health. I came across different methods for success that I found to be effective at making being successful in many areas all make sense. And, when I related these methods to my nursing knowledge of holistic wellness and our innate needs, my goals became even more organized. And so, I created the *heart of health*.

The heart of health describes your life in eight different areas that must balance in order to create contentment and happiness. Each area affects the balance of the whole system. The heart is a very helpful, simple way of organizing health and wellness because each area directly affects our physical and emotional health. Think of it as the shape of a heart from a bird's eye view; with each area an independent piece that is connected together to make a whole.

The eight areas are as follows: time, physical body, emotions and meaning, relationships, career, finances, contribution and spirituality. There are times when we go through certain life stages, like having kids or starting a new job, that we will focus more on certain areas while others are left aside. Though we can't always focus on each area at once, I like to have all the areas in my head so that I do not let any one of them go completely unattended. This allows me to create different goals to work toward in each area. I'll touch on each area now to give you something to think about that relates it to holistic care and the true meaning of wealth.

TIME

This is the ability to spend your time in a way that is most aligned with your values: spending time on family, hobbies, outdoor recreation, reading, travelling, or whatever it is you really enjoy doing. The ability and freedom to control our time should be what we all aspire to achieve. We should not be enslaved to a job we hate, have to miss important events, or have to say no to meaningful experiences because we don't have time. When you view time as an area of wealth, it may change the decisions you make about certain career choices. For example, you may feel you want to switch to a career that demands less of your time than your current job does.

Setting boundaries in this area is very important in order to separate work, family life, and finding enough time to spend on yourself. Once you find a way to control and create enough time to spend doing the things that fill your soul, you can consider yourself successful in this area of wealth.

PHYSICAL BODY

We discussed in an earlier chapter ways to obtain physical health, and it really is an area we must prioritize in order to obtain success in other areas. If you have ever dealt with an injury or complications from an illness, you will understand that healing and managing that pain requires most of your focus and energy. So, if you prioritize your physical health and are able to stay physically healthy, you will be able to focus your energy more on meeting life goals, maintaining and improving relationships, progressing your career, improving your parenting, exploring your creativity, and growing your soul.

EMOTIONS AND MEANING

As we have been discussing, mental health and wellness is as important as physical health. If your mind is not healthy, you will not want to focus on or improve any other area of your life. So, prioritize your mental health just as you do your physical health. Feeling hurt, happy, fearful, resentful, angry—all of it affects you and the way you conduct yourself, from your daily decisions to the way you feel in your day-to-day interactions.

Meaning refers to finding your purpose in life, which is something most people spend years trying to figure out. The more time you spend on meaningful experiences and developing your soul, the closer you get to ongoing feelings of fulfillment and contentment. This equals peace and happiness.

RELATIONSHIPS

This area of wealth involves everything that soothes your soul, as a life without belonging and companionship leads to loneliness and isolation. Everyone on earth has an innate desire for belonging and love, so this basic area of wealth is another absolute that must be paid attention to. Relationships are tricky though, because we spend our time trying to meet the needs of our loved ones without losing our sense of self. This area requires time and effort, but it pays off in unmeasurable amounts if you can successfully create, maintain and improve the relationships in your life.

Studies have shown that some of the main causes of depression are isolation and loneliness. You can avoid this by letting people into your heart and taking care of the people that mean the most to you. Don't make the mistake of spending the time you have here in this life alone.

CAREER

Whether it be a career outside of the home or one of staying at home to raise your children and tend to your family, your career is what the majority of your time is spent on. This is what makes this area so important.

If you are unhappy in your career, you will spend a lot of your time feeling this unhappiness, which in turn affects your overall mental wellness and emotional health. The career you choose must be something that meets the needs of your life and your soul. Maybe you choose it because it makes enough money to pay your bills, plan for your future, and take care of your family, which ultimately feeds your desire to provide. Or maybe you choose it because it is in a field that allows you to help people in the way that you crave doing.

Are you creative? Do you like to build things or generate new ideas? Maybe you love finance and studying financials and accounting. Maybe you like fixing things. Whatever it is, it is important that the kind of work you do fulfills your needs, both in practical life requirements and in soul growth. This area requires attention because you need to find happiness in the time you spend here in order to be successful.

FINANCES

Some people say money doesn't make the world go round. I disagree. You need money to survive. You need money to take care of yourself and your family. I am not one to rely on anyone else for anything, so the idea of letting the government or any other person take care of me financially sounds like a very dangerous path to walk and one that I'd recommend you to stop and consider. You never want to owe anyone anything. Let me say that again. You never want to owe anyone anything.

Independence means you can take care of yourself in all aspects of your life. It's OK to need assistance at times from family, friends, or the government system with which you live to help you along, but then you can pay it forward once you are out on the other side.

To be financially wealthy can mean many things to different people. For some, it can mean not having debt. For others, it means they can afford to pay their bills and feed their families. For others still, it means they do not live paycheque to paycheque, they have savings for their futures, they can afford entertainment and travel after all their bills are paid, they own land, or they have a million dollars. What does financial wealth look like for you? Think about this question, and then decide what you need to do to get there. Success in this area requires education, effort, and discipline, but it will be worth the sacrifices you may have to make now if it means you will be able to secure your financial state in the future.

CONTRIBUTION

It is my greatest belief that helping others is innate in us. In some people, they have lost the desire or ability to see past dark and live for the pure goodness that exists in each one of us. You cannot deny that helping someone that needs it, fills you up. It feeds your soul. It feels good. You wouldn't walk past an elderly person that just fell. You wouldn't step over someone that just dropped of a heart attack, you would call for help. Some of us hold doors for people, some of us offer hugs or condolences to someone that is grief stricken, some of us donate food to those that have nothing to eat. We all feel it. A desire to give back in some way. This is the biblical reference I think everyone has heard at some point in their life:

You shall love your neighbor as yourself – Leviticus 19:18.

Whatever your spiritual beliefs are, you know inside of your heart that being kind to others feels like the right thing to do. Doing good onto others fills up your soul. This is a natural part how we are designed, so make it part of who you are.

SPIRITUALITY

It is within this category that you may start to find a deeper meaning in your life and your purpose, and you may start to explore spirituality and the idea that the world is larger than just what we see here. It is within this category that people find true peace and contentment and develop a perspective that pulls them through the hardest of times. It is through spirituality that true gratitude is born.

Each of these areas is important, and each of these areas will have seasons where they are focused on more than others.

> *"You must gain control over your money or the lack of it will forever control you."*
> — Dave Ramsey

18.

MONEY TALKS

As we've already established, wealth doesn't just mean a bunch of money. To be completely balanced in contentment in all areas of our lives, we need more than just a bulging bank account. That being said, I am a big money fan. Money makes the world go around a lot more easily than it did in the earlier years of human existence. Think about the Dirty Thirties, war times, poverty worldwide, the days of hunting and gathering, the condition of human life before money was really invented.

Life was certainly a lot different back then. People had huge families, both from not having adequate means of birth control and the fact that fifty percent of children wouldn't survive due to a lack of adequate health care. People killed for survival. Families perished.

The increase in economic wealth throughout the world has introduced amazing advancements in technology and health care, and it has increased the quality of life for much of the human race that does not live in poverty. With the advantage personal financial stability, we have the option to survive without the need to destroy each other in a fight for food or shelter. Now, has this advancement stopped war? Not a chance, because power is still accessible and those that want it will continue to stop at nothing to get it. But the difference between the past and present times is that for those of us living in relatively stable economies where jobs, food, and shelter are available even in these crazy times of extreme costs of living, ongoing recessions, and massive national debts, we have the ability to meet our basic needs. When we are able to keep our families fed and safe, we can then begin to work on those later stages in Maslow's hierarchy of needs toward self-actualization.

It has been said that if you add money to whoever you are, it makes you a stronger you. So, if you are kind and you have a lot of money, you will remain kind while also becoming a stronger force in the world for helping others, as you will naturally choose to act kindly with said money. If you are greedy, mean, and angry, then with more money you will stay greedy and mean and become more dangerous with your anger as you will be able to use the power money can bring you for negative purposes. So, once an asshole, always an asshole. Does this make sense given your experience with assholes?

Very few people change these negative character traits within themselves because most have been created as a product of their environments, meaning, they come from having been deeply hurt. The thing about most angry people is that they do not wish to change or accept the state they live in, so they don't receive help in working through the emotions causing their toxicity. Undealt anger and sadness stay inside our bodies and eventually grow to become a toxic storm that can no longer be contained. This is where money becomes dangerous. You have all heard the saying, "money is the devil," but money is not the devil. The owner of the money is the one who controls its power.

Money is a blessing God allows us to use for the power of giving back. Those that are already kind and giving in nature and become very blessed in the area of finance use their money to help others in even more powerful ways than they could before. God trusts good stewards of money. If you give to others and help them in times of need, you will find the blessings keep coming back to you tenfold. Practise it. You'll see.

Money has an emotional hold on each of us. To properly understand why we view money the way we do, we must unpack the past and recognize the triggers that explain our money habits. Some develop a strong desire to obtain financial wealth because they grew up in a scarce environment. If their parents did not have money to buy food or pay the bills, then they either grew up and followed in the same path, or they developed a drive to never be in the same situation themselves. Some had parents who used money to buy love or forgiveness, some grew up wealthy and experienced judgment, some watched their mothers chose to stay home and raise babies before ending up with limited options after a failed marriage or maltreatment from her spouse, some had wealthy parents who used or misused the power they gained with their wealth. Everyone has a story related to money because it is the basis of all ability to survive.

I have a fear of debt. My fear comes from my childhood, where I watched my parents drink every time they talked about the stress of not having enough money and about the debt they held. I grew up on a farm, so our yearly income was dependent on the crop output for the year. Farming is a beautiful life, but like any business, it comes with unpredictability and a heavy weight on the shoulders of the business owner. I watched their drinking spiral out of control, and I attribute much of their addiction to their stressors, including feeling like they never had enough money.

Money creates power and power allows you to be independent. You do not want someone holding power against you, as those in serious financial strain experience from debt collectors and other people they depend on to meet their basic needs. Do not become reliant on anyone. You can't control the actions of people, so becoming dependent on someone puts you at risk of getting hurt.

Another important lesson we can learn from managing our finances is to be careful who you accept gifts from. Some people gift things or money from the bottoms of their kind hearts with absolutely no expectations of taking something back from you in return. But, some give with an ulterior motive, and this is something you must be very careful of. If you listen to your gut, you will be able to decipher between the two. Beware of those that hold expectations of return and that cause you guilt when such expectations are not met. As well, beware of those trying to manipulate you by using money or power. It is very important that you remain on high alert for people like this as you go through life, because manipulation can start subtly, and a skilled manipulator can trick you into straying from the truth of your internal value system.

Take the time to listen to your gut. Whatever your relationship is with money, think about your childhood and past experiences and start to make connections that explain why you feel and act as you do with money. You might be a spender or a saver, or you might be a bit of both. The spender may have been bought things to make them feel loved, or they may have low self-worth and feel like buying things makes them feel better. We all know how good it feels to buy clothes, furniture, houses, chocolate, wine, or a fine dining experience to soothe our high-riding emotions. But, whatever it is we buy, it's really nothing more than a Band-Aid. It feels good at first, but then the feeling wears down until you need to indulge again, to fill up your cup, to push the hurt back down, to soothe your pride. The saver doesn't want to spend because they are of a scarcity mindset and have a fear of not having enough money. These people come from backgrounds of scarcity and of needs not being met. If you have grandparents who were around for the Dirty Thirties, you will notice that today, in the twenty-first century, they still save leftover food far past when it should be eaten. They don't want to waste. I've known people that eat leftover ham three weeks after the cook date and set out mouldy buns to be consumed at mealtimes. Scarcity mindset. They don't want to throw anything out in case they maybe want to use whatever it is one day. Piles of junk? Well, maybe I'll want to build something one day with it. Hoarders. Oprah still saves her unfinished toast, so even people with much money can keep the traits of survival they developed in their pasts.

My dad was mean when he drank and the stress that money caused seemed to bring in more rum, which led to awful things in the aftermath. My mom drank to escape the stress because it was easier to numb it than to endure the pain. I wanted financial freedom because of what I saw my parents go through. I don't want the stress that comes along with not having enough money, because stress changes people, stress causes people to do terrible things, and stress breaks families apart. I made it my goal to avoid any of my past repeating itself by securing my future and the future of my loved ones to the best of my ability. Throughout their whole lives, I will teach my children the importance of having money and the options and opportunities that come along with it.

Striving for independence includes being able to pay for your own needs. Laziness is not an option for those that want more for themselves. Go hard to get it. Don't stop until you do. Most importantly, educate yourself. Read books, take courses, listen to podcasts. I suggest Dave Ramsey to teach the importance of debt management and Tony Robbins to educate on financial freedom options. *The Wealthy Barber* by Dave Chilton and *Rich Dad Poor Dad* by Robert Kiyosaki. What's most important is that you follow people that have paved their way to success in accordance with the values you hold or else it won't feel right in your gut. Their paths should resonate with you, your life goals, and the emotions you have attached to money management.

Stay honest, refrain from greed, give to those that are suffering, and prioritize your wants and needs. Always meet your basic needs before your wants—food, shelter, and safety must come first. Here are some other basic principles to follow:

1. *Pay attention to the money* coming in and money going out of your wallet and your accounts. Do not live your life unaware of where your money is. Use a tracking app such as EveryDollar for this and organize things so that every transaction is categorized.

2. *Develop a monthly budget* for your fixed and variable bills and stick to it. Within it, distinguish between needs and wants. Track this daily on an app like EveryDollar or something similar, which will help you see how much you are spending and on what. This knowledge will help you learn to control impulse buying.

3. *Do not compare yourself to others.* Let the Joneses spend all they want on all the things—your last name is not Jones (and if it is, then you are not part of *that* family). It is very important to remember that every

person has a different story. The Joneses may make a lot more money than you do, they may receive financial help from family, they may have won the lotto. Or, most likely, they just hold a lot of debt. From doing the math many times over while building my career and my family, I know that at the end of the day, you must use your common sense and just do the math. For those within your community, your utility bills will likely be similar. Interest rates on vehicles and other loans are usually similar. Mortgage rates, for every $500,000 spent, are always similar. Trips usually cost a similar amount of money. The cost of raising children is similar, and so on. So, stop comparing and do the math. It will leave you a lot less frustrated, especially when you don't know what other peoples' bank accounts and credit limits look like. Add business tax writeoffs and inheritance for some, and things get quite complex in the world of comparison.

Remember that many people are putting on a show to soothe their egos or to make up for a lack of self-worth. So, as you scroll through all of those highlight reels showing people going on another trip, or as you pass by that house or flashy SUV, or notice that girl with the hair extensions, lashes, manicured hands and feet, and designer everything, please remember that you do not know their story. On average, most that look rich are very, very broke. You would be surprised at how many people hold massive amounts of debt. Again, I'll say, to each their own.

4. *Eliminate debt if it makes you stressed.*
Your financial standing must be in alignment with your value system, so if you recognize that debt makes you feel stressed, then you need to get out of it. It is my very

strong opinion that we should not rely on or trust in others to look after us or our families. This is our job and we are the best equipped for it. When you are in debt, the person you owe money to holds power over you—this is what I want you to get far away from. Hear me loudly when I say that no one should hold any sort of power over you. So, to eliminate this chokehold, eliminate your debt.

Banks can change the interest rate on your loans and mortgages whenever they want, so when this happens, you will have no choice but to pay them more money. This is money being taken away from you and your family's financial freedom and quality of life. Do not let them control you. Pay off your debts. It is worth so much more to have the power of not having debt and having money in your bank account than it is to keep up with those fucking Joneses. I'm sick of them.

Make eliminating your debt your number one goal and attain it. It will take hard work, resilience, perseverance, struggle, focus, and tears. You will feel like a beaten warrior throughout the battle, but keep your long-term goal in mind and visualize every day what it feels like to have financial freedom from others controlling you. Your security and the security of your family depends on it. You can buy all the things you want later, once you have secured your future. Get your head above water before you take your foot off the gas. The release of stress that comes with being able to feel that freedom is worth every ounce of energy spent working to achieve it. It's worth every tear of exhaustion to get out of whatever mess you may be in.

5. *Find a balance.* In my line of work, I see too many people losing their lives or their health when they are way too young, stripping them of their ability to live as they had intended to. After all of the preaching I just did on debt management, I want to sprinkle a little message from the other side, just to add a little perspective and offer you the option to decide where to find your balance.

I suggest finding a balance between lifestyle and finances based on your value system, intuition, personal and family life goals, and passions. I know numerous people that do a lot of travel and have big houses and buy a lot of toys for their children. These types of people feel that there is time to save for retirement later. This is one way of thinking. Others value security more than anything to ensure safety and protection for themselves and their families. These types tend to not travel much, work overtime, and not overspend on houses and material possessions. It may be a less fun and different way of making memories while their kids grow up, but it is in exchange for peace of mind and financial security. So which way is wrong?

Listen, neither of these are wrong choices. It solely depends on how you want to live your life. I have always prioritized my financial future before material items or travel because I know what it feels like to be under someone else's control. The power to protect yourself financially is, to me, worth the short term sacrifice. Until you are financially prepared for the possibility of tragedy hitting your family, I feel you had best be choosing the costs of your enjoyment wisely. Memories can be made with little cost if you are creative and resourceful. We still camp in our 88' motorhome that my Grandpa gave us from when I was a little girl, because the kids absolutely love it and I love being squished in a small box when we are camping together. The vintage motorhome holds precious childhood memories for me and the small proximity adds so much value to the quality time we spend in there with each other. It's all about you, your experiences, your value system, your life goals, and what sits true in your heart. You just need to start asking yourself the questions and figuring out how you want to live.

6. *Meditate*. Call me a hippy, call me a spirit junkie, or call me crazy. I don't care. But you must attract what you want through the higher power and greater world around us that we cannot see. It is all about energy transfer and praying for guidance. Meditate on abundance and focus on money goals as if you have already reached them. Doing so will attract the energy to help you achieve your goals, but you must be sure to focus on the emotions around them. When you feel the emotions that will come with financial freedom, the ability to choose, and the capability for you and your family to live a better quality of life, you will attract the energy vibration from the invisible world around you, and these things will come to you. Just like when you have negative thoughts, you attract negative happenings. You won't understand until you know.

So, if you are open to crazy, do yourself a favour and just try meditating. Being an effective meditator won't happen overnight, so have faith in the process and learn how to do it. I'll say it again—it's not just you in your life, so pray. If you have faith, this I can promise you: guidance will come..

7. Have faith. It's time to get a little deep. Hey, I told you I hate small talk, so take my coffee chats as you wish. If you ever want to have a real conversation about real things and how you really feel, I am a huge lover of this kind of chat. Give me all the real stuff—don't hide behind fear of judgment with me. If you have ever read the Dalai Lama, you will understand that connecting with someone, getting to understand someone better, and learning about other people's journeys has much to do with connection. It has nothing to do with judgment about the uncontrolled environment that fuels most of our decisions anyway. It's all about the person inside of that ego. The ego trying to survive the rat race in this world. So here it goes. To another area of wealth worth exploring.

I am a firm believer in a higher power, and my faith in God and his plans for us is very true to my heart. For those of you that have experienced God reaching out to you, I need not explain the feelings that swirl in your stomach and the peace and love that fill your heart when you touch the spirit world. For most who have truly felt this and had their faith confirmed, it unfortunately tends to happen after hardship. "Find Me in the River," a song written by Martin Smith, describes this as sometimes having to walk through storms in order to see light. It is why we have to battle. One thing I have come to understand is that with human error in free choice or unexplained trauma and loss, if we open our hearts, our higher power will carry us through.

The bigger picture and the learning journeys of each of our souls is larger than you can imagine. After you endure hardship, you have the ability to truly feel joy once more. You feel gratitude on a much deeper level, you feel peaceful knowing you are safe. If you never experience the emotions associated with adversity, how could you truly know joy? How could you truly feel peace? You don't understand these things until you experience the emotions of hurt, resentment, anger, fear, loss, suffering... and from those lessons, a much stronger you is created.

As a nurse, I have had the honour of holding space for those at the end of their lives and being present with them in their journeys crossing over. I can promise you that the unique facial expressions, deep breaths, or gasps of surprise during these passings assures me that there is more to this life than our human existence in our physical forms on this earth. So, while you are here, find your faith in whatever it is you find sits peacefully in your heart—it can be spiritual, religious, or both. Either way, you must do the work in finding where your faith lies.

My faith is Christian-based, but my heart serves the spiritual world. I have studied different people who believe opposing aspects of what God wants from us. If you get confused on this topic and need simplification, I suggest you read *Teachings of Silver Birch,* edited by A.W Austen. If you believe in life after death, heaven, and angels, Silver Birch describes God as the higher power and simplifies all religions into the true meaning of life for all human forms. This book will help it all make sense for you. The great laws he talks of are so simple—they are things that we already innately know. Being kind to one another is one of his greatest lessons. His main teachings cover the same teachings as the Bible, but with different wording. Choose what resonates most with you. If you are comfortable and craving to put your faith in a religion, pick up a bible and start reading. You will find what you need once you start looking.

We must understand that a life without so much hurt can be so simple to obtain if we could all see life from a different perspective. Look around you. People are in their own little worlds where things happen to them and they become victims. I am here to help you see that you are not a victim of what has been done to you. You are larger than that. Stronger than that. You will learn forgiveness and that will set you apart. These areas of wealth are what I want you to understand so that you can incorporate all the pieces to make you whole.

8. *Give to fill your heart.* A life of enjoyment is not one to feel shameful of. God wants us to live life freely and feel joy in our day-to-day. If you are a good steward of his money, because it is his as everything in this world is, you will feel greatly content inside. Spend your life giving to others, just as you enjoy reaping the benefits of your hard work for yourself and for your family. You will feel excited to have the power to help someone out of an awful situation if your heart comes across the opportunity. With this act will come blessings and greater abundance.

Try it if you do not believe me. Read about it. When you start to live with an abundant mindset rather than a scarcity mindset, you will find abundance starts flowing to you. Open your heart, give to others in ways that you find fill your heart, and watch what happens.

People talk about karma and how what you give out comes back to you. I am 100% a believer in this. I've watched it happen enough times to know now that when someone is mean or someone is greedy, they will never find real peace and contentment until they change. In the end, they will have to take it up with the man upstairs, and I feel sorry for them. They will have to face the consequences and the shame one day, and they will experience loneliness and hardship, loss of relationships and hurt. I also know that bad things can happen to good people too—it is all part of a world we can't understand. But, there is more out there, and the spirit world is so powerful. So, listen to your soul, and be kind to others. You will not regret it.

*"You cannot save people,
you can just love them."*

— Anaïs Nin

19.

COMPLEXITY IN RELATIONSHIPS

Loneliness causes depression. We are born to belong with each other. Belonging is one of the human needs in that good old hierarchy of needs pyramid I keep harping on about. It is number three, after physiological and safety needs. Love and belonging. It's so important.

I wanted first to help guide you to becoming completely independent, not having to rely on anyone. But while you work toward this, and forever after reaching it, I want you to also work on the area of relationships, because a strong support system and a full heart turn the strength you have already harnessed into a superpower. Your soul needs other souls to be fulfilled, and your heart needs to love as much as it needs to be loved.

Let's talk about being single, being in a relationship, marriage, friendships, and family.

To have a friend that understands your hurt without judgment, that needs not compare their lives to yours but rather stands beside you while you walk your path, that cares enough to listen with or without offering up solutions depending on what you are looking for—that is a saving grace for the soul. It allows you to be independent without being alone, to have companionship and connection without losing yourself.

For those that have chosen to be alone, when you look into their eyes, you can see loneliness and unfulfillment right in their souls. They have chosen to be alone because of Debilitating fear, lack of confidence and self-worth, and lack of willingness to try anything else because they don't even know what they are missing. Does any of this sound familiar to you?

If you start to study people, you will find that many are lonely, even when they are in relationships. I know you have all felt this way at one time in your lives or another, or maybe you feel it very much today and it is one of the reasons you found this book. You are in a relationship that you are maybe not happy in right now. You are lonely inside of that relationship. Those of you that seek friends on a deeper connection level: you are lonely. Once you can recognize this about yourself and admit it, then you can gain the courage to fix it.

There are times in your life when you need to be alone—times to not be in a relationship, times to not seek a partner. It is in these times that your soul needs to build independence and strength on its own and heal its hurts without anyone else affecting the process or taking away from the attention and energy required to repair the damage inside. If you listen to your body, you will be able to understand when these times are. You will know when you must shut out the outside world and focus your energy on you. In these times, you will naturally feel more introverted.

Have you ever noticed that our eyes are the window to our souls? Have you ever been able to see sadness when you look at someone and know how they are feeling without them having to say it? Study people that are unfulfilled. Look into their eyes. Look into a mirror. Recognize the look. Once you reach inner contentment, you will notice a change in the eyes looking back at you. This is very important in attaining self-worth. Once you start to see that change in your eyes, you will have reached self-actualization—contentment without perfection—the ability to be OK in any situation because you have the battle gear stored inside of you. Your support network can make a world of difference in helping you reach this level, but only healthy support is invited or else you will struggle in your journey. Once you reach self-actualization, you will attract all kinds of people! It will be amazing to experience.

DATING

Dating is hard. Period. I don't care who you are or what age you are—dating is hard. And here's why.

People are crazy.

Seriously.

There are so many different types of people in this world, and you are trying to find one that aligns with the kind of person you are and that suits your character traits. In particular with online dating, you sometimes find people who only want sex and they can sure be forward and disrespectful in requesting it. To all of you that have experienced this, you can immediately let these people go from your mind and do not let them affect your sense of self-worth because they are facing an inside problem that has nothing to do with you. You are the one who decides how you should be treated, so do not interact with anyone speaking to you in any sort of manner that doesn't make you feel calm and happy in your gut. If someone says something that makes that makes you wrinkle your forehead, it is not appropriate. That frown wrinkle is a natural response to the dumb things people and say and do, and I tell you, mine has gotten very deep! Seriously, zoom in on a picture of me and you'll see it. Save yourself the Botox bill and listen to my words. Everyone is battling some sort of demon, everyone has had different life experiences, and everyone has had different upbringings with different sets of values (or a lack thereof). Keep yours aligned and don't put up with anyone's shit. Period.

Another reason why dating is hard? Because you're trying too hard. Most people do when they want something so badly, right?

I'm going to get all hippy on you again and make you think for a second about your thought process when you are longing for something. When you want something so much, you constantly think about how you lack that thing. I really want a boyfriend... I really want a relationship... I really want to be a wife... I really want to be in love and have someone hold me, care for me, and be there for me... I really want passion like I see in the romance movies I watch... You get the picture? I really want, so I don't have. So, I am lonely, sad, frustrated, depressed without. Instead of this kind of thinking, I want you to visualize already having the love of your life. Describe him or her, put the qualities he or she possesses on a vision board—qualities that make you feel loved, respected, and cared for. Focus on how it would feel once you have found love. This is all part of the manifesting process, which can't be believed until you've tried it. It really is life-changing if you can just open your mind to the possibility of a whole other world existing aside from this earth life. The way I see it though, is what do you have to lose by trying it? It certainly won't hurt to try it every day and adapt a new, healthy practice through meditation.

The most important thing I want to touch on about romantic relationships is your self-worth. You must first figure out how you deserve to be treated before you can be happy in any relationship, so learning how to detect red and yellow flags in the dating world is imperative. On my self-worth journey, it took numerous lessons for me to finally understand how valuable I am, so I let a lot of relationships play out even though they never should have gone farther than a few dates. I know I am not alone in those experiences. There are too many young girls and guys out there that don't understand how to be properly treated, so I want you to tune in and hear my words loudly here.

In all relationships, we must first and foremost develop a strong value system. I know, I know, I say this with every topic in health and healing, but this is because your values are literally your internal compass for every decision you make in life. In regards to dating, you must start thinking about how you feel you deserve to be treated. The answer here is going to be different for everyone because a) everyone has a different soul with different personality traits related to tolerance and b) everyone has had different life experiences. What one person may tolerate could be something someone else would never even think of putting up with. This tolerance will change as you grow and change throughout the seasons of your life.

Let's start with high school. During high school is when we are all just trying to figure out who we are. I spent much time in the small town I lived in walking the quiet streets with all different groups from school. I was a farm girl in a Walmart sweat suit or jeans and t-shirt, hair pulled back in a pony, riding quads and go-karts, cuddling my four-hundred-pound pet pig I saved from being the runt of the litter that my dad wanted to get rid of, and yes, I named her Wilbur, and yes, I put her in the town parade. Then I was a punk with short, spiky hair who wore really baggy pants and listened to Beck a lot. After that I was part of the pretty-girl club, with an interest in fashion and style, longer hair, not going a day without make-up, flirting with a lot of boys, and going to all the parties. It can be hard to tell who you actually are, so you have to try out all the ways of expressing yourself. No? Just me?

OK, it took me a while to figure myself out, but given an unstable father/daughter relationship, I guess you could expect me to be quite unsure of who I really was. But, let's be honest here—you could have the best relationship with your dad and still fall for a guy that hurts you and stomps on your self-worth. In fact, I think most young people do go through this. I've even watched my son go through a couple of heartbreaks and saw how very quickly he learned to put up his guard. Being young is tough. Learning is tough.

In my high school years, I dated two guys. One guy was a genuinely good guy, and the other was a piece of shit. He used me, cheated on me, and showed very poor character in life in general. My mom and dad used to get so mad when he would come over after school because he would sit inside the house while I went out and did two hours of chores in minus thirty Alberta weather. When I got in from chores, he was always waiting for me to make him something to eat. He got hungry you know, waiting inside for me to finish up feeding the pigs.

If you pay attention to people's small characteristics, you will see that they are a window into the bigger character traits. This same guy dated me and someone else at the same time, playing

COMPLEXITY IN RELATIONSHIPS

us with lies. He happened to belong to one of the most popular groups in school, so as a young, high-school girl with no self-worth trying to gain it through external sources, it was easier to fall for his bullshit. Sound familiar to anyone?

I also ended up cheating on the nice guy with that loser because I was so under his spell and didn't understand that my self-worth didn't come from impressing people or being in the most popular group in high school. If you are making decisions that are not aligned with your value system because of someone else, this is a clue that you need to get them out of your life. The person you are with should make you a better person—they should not lead you to make regrettable decisions or change who you are inside.

As I moved into my twenties, I found a group of guy friends that I hung out with all the time. There were six of them. We did everything together, and they protected me through every day. They were my team of guys that made me feel cherished and loved. This is where I started to find value in myself. Some of the best years of my younger days were spent hanging out with these boys, but through these times, I kept choosing players and assholes to date. Each of my friends went through a stage where they wanted our friendship to turn into something more, but I had put them all in the friend zone because I was not willing to lose the way they made me feel as my good buddies if our relationship turned sour. But, the other truth was that I was not attracted to them because they were too nice to me. Sound familiar? This happens all the time. Girls look for guys that will treat them how they feel they deserve to be treated. The stupid thing about this is that it is all done subconsciously as we move into each experience not thinking about why we make the choices we do. My guy friends would ask why I kept dating guys that kept using me and playing games with me. I never had a true answer. I didn't know why. I just knew I was attracted to them.

Well, I'm here to put a stop to that ignorance. To all of you of any age out there: when you have a low self-worth, you will be naturally attracted to people that mistreat you. I've mentioned this old saying before, that girls look for the qualities of their fathers in the men they choose to date, and it is absolutely a true statement that we must be very aware of. It is how the cycle of abuse keeps continuing. And you don't need to have been abused by your father to have low self-worth—people can damage your self-worth with their mean-ness and judgment just the same, but on a different scale. So, until you learn how to develop self-worth, you need to be aware that you are following a subconscious pattern of tolerating what you think you are worthy of.

There are a few simple rules you should follow as you maneuver through the dating world. These go for anyone at any age.

1. *Create a set of values.* Make a list of the character traits you value in people and in yourself. This is a unique, personal list that is specific to only you. Some examples are as follows: honesty, integrity, reliability, kindness, genuineness, personability, interactivity, adventurousness, security, hardworking nature, financial responsibility, fun-loving nature, romantic nature, passion, drive, emotional stability. These are traits you admire in people and that you would like your partner to have as they travel next to you along your life path. These are traits that align with your character and that will make it easier to go through life events together later, such as having children, building a secure financial foundation, travelling, educating, dealing with loss, dealing with people, handling life challenges, etc. No

one is perfect, so you will never find a perfect match to your list, but you can choose which traits you find most important and find someone that aligns with these.

A very important trait to look for in someone is a willingness to compromise and communicate. If someone is not willing to look outside themselves, blames the world for their problems, or angers easily and feels a sense of entitlement, beware that a relationship with them could require a lot of work. You need to find someone humble and confident enough to be willing to change and grow as they pass through life—because that is you. I know this about you, because you never would have picked up this book if this wasn't you.

2. *Make a list of boundaries.* Look inside to determine your value system and from there set healthy boundaries of what behaviours you are willing and not willing to put up with. My list of boundaries has changed over the course of my dating life as well as my married life. This is what they look like at this time:

> A. *I will not tolerate abuse* of any sort—this includes physical, verbal, or manipulative abuse. This is number one for me because I have experienced all three types of abuse and I will never accept that behaviour for myself ever again, nor will I ever subject my children to receiving that kind of behaviour.
>
> B. *I will not tolerate* someone who is not willing to work toward financially security. I am hardworking by nature, and financial security for me and my family is imperative. I will not spend my life with someone who is lazy and unwilling to contribute

to our family's financial safety. I believe in a team mentality in relationships, and carrying someone while they take advantage of my work ethic and kindness is not something I am willing to put up with. If someone becomes unable to work during the course of our relationship, then of course that is a whole different scenario and I would gladly carry them on my back. But, love, effort, respect, and teamwork need to be proven first before I do this for someone.

C. *I will not tolerate* an unwillingness to change and grow throughout the seasons of life. This will not work for me because I am always looking to learn and grow, to become stronger and wiser, and to continue through life by adapting to inevitable change. If I do not have a partner willing to do the same, then we will not be able to stay on the same path and it will become far too difficult later to maintain a healthy relationship.

D. *I will not tolerate* someone who is selfish and unkind. Period.

3. *Listen to your intuition.* It never betrays you. When you start dating someone, especially now with online dating being the number one way to find someone, it can be very easy for people to be superficial and dishonest about who they are. Tread lightly in getting to know people and watch for signs that someone's character is off. If you sense a red or yellow flag for behaviour that doesn't match the value system you have created, then don't bother continuing the relationship. These flags you get are a glimpse of your inner compass letting you know that something is not right.

COMPLEXITY IN RELATIONSHIPS

All of this being said, some things are worth fighting for. You must look inside yourself and dissect the situation based on what you know of the person, and make your choice from there. If you see life as black and white, then you will have an easier time with this. For others who see a lot of grey, this won't be as easy. If you are still working on your self-worth and confidence and need help with following your intuition, use your respected mentors to sound off for advice. If you have yet to find a mentor, keep following my work, as healing others has become a huge part of what I do. Live in the now, but think about the future. It is so important to live in the present time with who you are today and how you feel in this season of your life. One thing to always keep in the back of your mind, however, is how your future self will feel about the decisions you make today.

When you date someone, think of the person they are today as well as who they have the potential to be in the future. For example, if you want to have kids one day and the boy you are dating seems immature but he has the base characteristics of being a reliable partner and he also wants a family in the future, then there is a good chance that he can grow into being the man you hoped for for your future self. The same goes for the guys out there—if the girl you are dating seems kind at heart, caring, and matches the values you hold, let go of some of the immature choices they may make. These experiences may border on the coloured flags line, so again, just look within yourself, and your gut will help you decipher if their current behaviour is something you can live with right now and in the future.

One thing we know is that it is impossible to change other people. So, you must choose someone based on whether you are willing to love them despite the things you cannot change. A friend once told me that before she got married, she and her fiancé received traditional, Christian, pre-marriage counselling sessions to discuss matters that are important and sacred to the bond of marriage. In one session, they were asked to choose one thing about each other that they didn't like. My friend's fiancé chose smoking for her. The counsellor asked him if he was willing to marry her as a smoker, because only she could decide whether to quit one day; he could not force her to. He had to choose then and there whether to end the relationship because of it, or to take her as she was, even as a smoker. He chose to take her as she was, just as she chose to take him as he was. Neither party brought forward any resentment, nor did they force change onto each other, even for their unadmirable qualities. They got married. She quit smoking. Take the qualities you see in your potential partner and consider them in the same way my friend and her fiancé had to.

4. *Choose someone* that makes you a better person. When you spend enough time with some people, certain qualities of theirs can bring out other qualities in you. The proximity principle, which states that we become more like the closest people around us, is true, and it especially includes our partners because we spend so much time with them.

You will have heard that opposites attract, and I do agree with that, but not in every case. Some people look for others that are much more like themselves. I am a combination of both. My husband and I have many similar traits, but a few are polar opposites. He is strong and assertive, loud and opinionated, fiery and unaccepting of stupidity. This is the opposite of me. I am quiet and passive, empathetic and submissive, laid-back and forgiving. Different personalities, neither of which is better or worse. But his strong qualities have been a God-send in my self-worth journey. He has been behind me and coached me through many scenarios, empowering me and showing me what I should and shouldn't be tolerating. He brings the fire out in me, and I bring the calm back to him. Being opposites works in our case.

You must find someone that helps make you a better person. A toxic person on the other hand will form you into someone who is not aligned with your soul, and that will lead to a lifetime of struggle.

5. *Do not settle.* This is the most important thing to remember when you are dating. Don't settle with someone you think might be OK just because you are tired of looking or are too impatient to wait. They say life is short, but life can be really long if it is spent with someone you are not aligned with. Take your time. There are billions of people in the world. Get out of your comfort zone, try new things, put yourself in situations where you meet new people through your career or extracurriculars, don't let fear debilitate you from talking to someone you really want to approach, take deep breaths, keep your values in check, and enjoy the ride.

INSIDE A RELATIONSHIP

Relationships are complex. We need them to complete our souls, but finding the wrong person to spend our lives with is detrimental. The decisions we make to choose partners, figure out how to create lives with them, then choose to stay with them or leave them are huge. I say this in complete honesty because life in the twenty-first century is not the same as it once was. If you talk to our elderly population, you'll know it was once out of the question to leave your marriage. It wasn't even an option; you stayed no matter the circumstances. A marriage vow was a declaration of lifetime commitment, through good times and bad, in sickness and health, till death do us part.

Through nursing, I have had the chance to hear some extremely interesting relationship stories from the older generation. Every time I meet a couple that has celebrated fifty-plus years of marriage together, I ask them what their secret to a successful relationship is. Every answer is different, though most are along the lines of always communicate, always respect each other, keep loving each other no matter what, think about the other person when making choices, choose each other first, and so on. An interesting answer my grandmother once gave me was, "Just let him do whatever he wants to keep himself happy, like play sports, play music, go places, and do the things he wants to do. It's easier that way." Hmmm. I understand what she was saying here, in that my grandfather loves people, always wants to be socializing at dances and such, and loves to do things like camp, fish, and play music every weekend with his Old-time country band. My grandmother was more of an introvert, and while she did always attend the dances and do the things my grandfather wanted to do, it was at the expense of who she was and what she wanted to be doing. She was an amazing caregiver, and I believe she truly loved caring for her kids and grandkids and being a farmwife and homemaker, but I believe she lost the rest of who she was in the art of pleasing.

Women now are taking on major careers and fighting for equality and empowerment, no longer content to just hold their posture and keep their lips pursed throughout a lifetime of pleasing their spouses. Feminism has provided women with the confidence

COMPLEXITY IN RELATIONSHIPS

and ability to fight for how we should be treated. Through this progression of women's rights, the divorce rate has increased, a change that we see in present time to be directly correlated to the change in the way we think men and women should coexist compared to years ago. So, the vow of marriage has actually become quite complicated. No longer are people willing to tie themselves to a life not worth living.

Where do you stand in this? Do you think you should endure any and all things to keep the sanctity of the marriage bond intact? Or should you choose yourself and a lifetime of happiness over a person who is not providing you with the life you wanted?

I'll tell you where my faith lies.

The complexity of marriage is person-specific. You cannot base the fate of a relationship on a religious rule or a traditional way of thinking. It is solely a you choice based on your relationship, family unit, value system, and life experience. Some people end up cheating in their marriages. I watched this happen on separate occasions to good friends. I do not agree with being unfaithful, but I did witness the events that led up to these people landing in the headspace they were in before committing infidelity. I am a strong believer in the old saying that it takes two. It takes two to have a failed marriage, it takes two to make a baby (unless you are raped), it takes two to make a lifelong, committed relationship work while life changes both of you.

As we know, everything changes. When people change, it causes all sorts of issues within an intimate relationship, which I do not believe can be judged by anyone on the outside looking in. Some feel, as they examine their own actions that contributed to their spouse's desire to have their needs met elsewhere, that second and third chances are warranted. For others, cheating is a deal-breaker. People tolerate different levels of abuse, and some tolerate none at all and couldn't fathom why anyone else would either. Some choose to stay in a changed, unfulfilling marriage because they don't want to hurt their children by leaving. Some believe it is better for their children if they do leave, because the effects of being around an unsuccessful relationship may end up hurting their children worse in the long run. Some look at the logistics of what separation would entail and choose to stay together for financial reasons or to manage the children's schedules in a roommate/teamwork approach. Some never leave because they are scared. So complicated.

Where does your heart sit in this? Are you happy in your relationship? Are you happy most days, or very few? Is your partner willing to communicate with you, even as they navigate through life events and emotional volatility? Are you willing to communicate with them?

One thing I know is that relationships go through seasons like everything else. Seasons of lust and passion, romance, stagnancy, excitement, hardship, routine, and hurt. When you first enter a relationship, you each make a strong effort to please each other, to tantalize each other, to impress each other, and earn each other's trust. You find it fun to spark desire in the other person, and life seems light and exciting. As the relationship moves forward, you begin to learn new things about each other and your comfort level around each other increases so that each person begins to show a truer side of themselves. Once a certain level of comfort is reached, the relationship enters a new level of seriousness and devotion. It is in this stage that you begin to experience challenges, stronger disagreements, and trouble communicating through new emotions, but the level of dedication you have to each other causes you to want to last through these hardships, as opposed to giving up and leaving.

COMPLEXITY IN RELATIONSHIPS

This is why it has been said that if you can make it through the first seven years of your relationship, then chances of it lasting a lifetime increase substantially. Most divorces happen during this initial seven-year period, as couples transition through the highest learning curve for how to love each other through life's happenings. A lot of people change or build careers, have babies, deal with the loss of aging parents or others they love, or battle financial stress during this period.

My husband and I have been together for thirteen years and the amount that we have learned about each other in dealing with life events and storms together has been astronomical. We started out in two very different places in life. He was young at heart, his main goal in life was to have fun, he had no knowledge of finance nor had any reason to learn, and he had been hurt by girls in the past, which had caused him to put up a very large wall of distrust. I was an old soul raising a little boy on her own, with a history full of storms and abuse I had endured. I was stubborn though, and had learned how to stand tall so that none of my war wounds showed. (In fact, I had so many scars that I didn't even know the actual wounds still existed deep inside of me. That lovely surprise came later.) I was hardworking and financially driven to support my precious boy, but I didn't have a huge knowledge base when it came to finance. I just knew what I had been taught at the time.

Has our relationship always been easy? Lord, no. There were many times when I thought we were in big trouble, mostly because I had changed so much from the person I was when he met me. I believe God brought us together for many reasons and I believe very much in timing. The tolerances I had then are not at all what I have now, but he helped empower me to make those changes. He has a completely different wife today than he did then. He once had a passive, submissive, people-pleasing, no-boundaries, can-take-care-of-everyone-and-everything-and-still-be-fine-no-matter-what wife. That's who I had been. Amazing actually, but I was broken inside, and I didn't even know it until it all knocked me down one day. I have an even greater strength deep inside of me, because I have boundaries and self-respect now, so things look a lot different. Lucky for me, my husband was able to deal with the huge changes in me, and lucky for him, I stuck around while he figured out how to become the man he has grown into. A kind, caring, protective man.

I'm going to simplify how to create a successful relationship into five important areas to focus on. Just remember as we go through them that each person has their own unique qualities based on their values and life experiences that will affect whether they decide to stay and fight to keep a person, or to leave and move on without them. Here are the five things to focus on in order to help your relationship withstand all the storms and last through the good and the bad.

1. *Communication*. This is the lungs of your relationship—it's ability to breathe. It is an essential part of a healthy relationship. You must find your voice, choose the right times to have certain conversations, and listen when your partner needs to say something. If you can't breathe, you cannot survive.

2. *Respect*. This is the backbone of your relationship. Without respect for one another, your relationship has no spine and it will crumble. Respect means many things to different people, but to keep it simple, here it means listening to your partner's needs, not practising selfishness as your partner matters as much as you do, and treating your partner how you would want to be treated at all times.

3. *Boundaries*. This is the musculoskeletal system of your relationship. The connective tissues. You need boundaries in your relationship and within yourself to keep proper strength and connection for stability and health. When you allow toxicity to enter you or your relationship, you lose the ability to maintain the strength you need to endure the challenges. You become weak. You must keep your connective tissues and muscles strong to protect your body—your relationship. Practise strength training.

4. *Understanding*. This is the endocrine system of your relationship. It is the hormones created by your glands to control all of your bodily functions, from metabolism, growth and development, fertility and sexual function, and sleep, to kidney function, digestion, and blood pressure. It makes the body work. It is understanding your partner, what they may be feeling, what they may have felt in the past, what internal battles they may be struggling with, why they have trouble with communicating or meeting other expectations, why they do the things they do, and why they are the way they are. Understanding them makes the relationship work. Allow room for empathy and understand them from the inside out. This will allow for proper functioning.

5. *Love*. This is literally the heart of your relationship. Never stop loving each other. That's it. As long as your heart has a beat, your relationship is alive.

FOR THE LOVED AND LOST

If you have ever loved and lost, you know right away what I mean when I say the process is a rollercoaster of emotions and grieving, and a struggle with self-worth, especially through the initial impact of the loss. A broken heart from a breakup in your younger years involves introspection on who you are, why you feel you are not enough, and what made things go wrong. These early broken hearts seem detrimental to us at the time because we are still emotionally maturing and learning to regulate the whirlwind of emotions we feel from reactions to life events so big that we feel like life is over. Life events so big that we feel like we will never get over them. And, well, you never really do get over them in a way. It gets easier as time passes, but the sting will never be forgotten. Sometimes we need the sting to learn the life lesson, but it doesn't make the process any easier. A broken heart from divorce will always hold grief in regards to loss of identity and loss of the dream you once had when you made vows on the day you married this person.

Married or not, breakups hurt, period. For those of you going through one, you can understand that the path of grief is like climbing the same mountain you must climb with any loss. You'll have good days and bad, and a lot of tears will fall. What I want you to focus on here is the self-worth aspect of the loss. Give yourself grace in this healing period and take time to reflect on and decipher how each of you played a part in making your relationship go wrong. I am not a fan of the victim card, so you won't get any validation from me if you point all of the blame to the other party. It always takes two for a relationship to fail, so the important part is for you to understand what you might have done wrong so that you can carry this learning forward into your next relationship. And yes, there will be a next eventually, so this is an essential practice for our own learning, growth of emotional maturity, and spiritual reveal.

If you look back at your history of broken relationships, it is often easier to detect what your current self would change about your past self now than it is to in the moment. Maybe it was boundaries you should have set, maybe you were not good at communicating for one or more of the millions of reasons that people struggle with communication (that's a whole book in itself because communication is such a complex tool tied to so many past experiences and encounters with people, trauma, self-worth, fear, and so much more), maybe it was your underdeveloped emotional regulation, or maybe it was that life happened and your partner changed into someone you couldn't grow to love anymore. Whatever it was, figure it out, because that information is like gold going into your future relationships.

Do you want to know the secret that nobody ever tells you as you enter your dating life? The one thing you must actually know and truly believe before you can ever have a successful, healthy relationship? Listen closely, because it's something you can never forget: **Before you can love anyone else, you must genuinely love all parts of yourself first.** That is the secret.

It's doesn't seem that hard of a concept to understand, does it? But actually believing it and doing it in real life is a lot harder than saying it on paper. So, as you are reflecting, I want you to think about all of the things that happened to you in your failed relationships that you feel you didn't deserve. Write them down. And let the ugly cry out while you do it. Chances are, you deserved so much better than how you were treated, or talked to, or listened to. Be extra kind to yourself during the healing time after this breakup because your soul has been hit. It will feel like a battle wound, and you need tender loving care. That's the heart of the truth. If the same were happening to your sister, brother, friend, daughter, son, father, or mother, you would love them extra hard now because you would know that their heart needed it and that they didn't deserve to be treated in the way they maybe were. So, do me a favour, and treat yourself how you would treat a loved one with a broken heart. After time has passed and you begin to feel a little more whole again, start the process of self-reflection so that you can carry your learnings into your next relationship, whenever you feel ready to do so.

Just don't ever forget the secret. Learn to love yourself before you let someone else in.

"Let me ask you something. If someone prays for patience, you think God gives them patience? Or does he give them the opportunity to be patient? If they prayed for courage, does God give them courage, or does he give them opportunities to be courageous?"

— Morgan Freeman, *Evan Almighty*

20.
DRAWING THE LINES

This will change your whole world in a matter of seconds. That's all it takes. Less than a minute for a complete life change, and a complete internal change. Call it the secret to a life you never thought was possible.

Boundaries. Sounds so simple, doesn't it? Well, I tell you what, it really is simple. But practising it? Dealing with the emotions that go along with the practise? Possibly the hardest things you'll ever do in your life. But it's all about letting go... so let's let go.

This chapter is about property lines and how they will save you at the same time as they will end you. Now, I'm not talking about ending you like Gerard Butler taking down a White House full of bad guys in order to save the president, but this kind of ending does have the same brilliant finish. By the way, that man is so sexy. Anyway, learn where your boundaries lie, and you will find peace. But the test that comes with practising boundaries is the hardest. I'm talking about the guilt you will feel when you learn to say no and witness the real-time disappointment of your loved ones as you stand up to them. Some will not like the new you, and you will lose them. Some will adjust, but the guilt and shame they lay on you will is what you must practise letting go of. The tricky thing is that it all ties in with the inner workings of your core, built from day one of you exiting the womb.

Every encounter and every person that has had an impact on you in some way lies in a marked file deep in that pretty brain of yours, and oh boy does it hurt to let go of who you used to be in the process of becoming who you need to be. It becomes part of a grieving process because you are literally saying goodbye to the person you once were. We all know how hard the grieving process is, so you can imagine even before you start how many hard days there will be in the making of a new you. But, you must keep in mind why you are changing you—why it's a matter of life and death, actually. You must remember that you cannot keep going the way you have been going: continuing to let others control the emotions that course through your body and the choices you make in reaction to those emotions. It has to stop! You are no longer going to constantly put everyone else's needs in front of yours, and especially not the needs of those who have been mean to you. Continuing to live this way will destroy you. It's done now. What you will find out is that you possess a strength you never thought possible. You alone have the ability to change how others treat you—all those that have disrespected you, guilted you, hurt you, and used you. We'll get through this one together. I've got your back. First though, you must know that you're not alone.

If you have had some sort of trauma in your past the inside of you remembers all too well, and it makes it harder for you to say no to people and things. This is PTSD at its finest: when it is in the most hidden and unexpected places. That inner child that lives in you still fears the person who caused you trauma. If you just avoid upsetting that person and all people, then you can avoid danger and keep yourself safe. You learn to conform so that other people won't get mad. You tiptoe around the world so that you can stay safe. You are hyperaware of anyone that has the potential to lash out, and you learn how to please these people so that the alarms ringing inside of you quiet back down. We all know what happens when those alarms go on ringing—terror and hurt follow—and we do anything to avoid this. Too many times we've had to hide and please. Too many times we've had to avoid saying the word that lights a fire in their eyes.

FOR THOSE THAT LEARNED TO PLEASE

People pleasing is an art. A true form of expression for millions avoiding conflict and the disappointment of others. You don't have to have endured major trauma to have acquired this talent. You simply have to have felt unloved in some way, and then tried to adapt your behaviors to achieve a sense of belonging. It's also a safety mechanism. You unconsciously believe that if people like you, they can't get mad at you, which keeps you out of harm's way. If people like you, they won't shame you or express disappointment in the person you are. If people like you, maybe you can learn to start to like yourself.

In the art of pleasing people, you will lose sight of who you really are, and what you really enjoy. The reactive urge to ensure everyone else around you is comfortable means you live in a superficial state. Once you find the courage to put your needs in front of others, an inner feeling of trust for yourself begins to develop. This is the beginning of the transformation to acquiring self-worth and feeling a genuine love for the person you are. It takes a lot of practise, and you will feel selfish at first. Those around you that have known you to be a people pleaser will name you selfish, as they have been accustomed to having you conform to their ideologies and needs before your own. The secret is, that those people you need to set boundaries with are the ones that have been taking advantage of you. Compare those relationships with others in your life that you have never needed to set those boundaries with. Those that have respected you, valued you, and acknowledged your feelings do not require boundaries, because they have already established them in their love and respect for you. Notice the difference? Now remember that when you work on this people pleasing habit of yours.

STOP APOLOGIZING

You deserve space in this world. You deserve to walk on your side of the path, and you deserve to be heard when you have something you wish to say. Too many times we walk around apologizing to anyone and everyone that almost walks into us, or that doesn't want to hear what we have to say. Well if they run into you, why are you saying sorry? If they don't want to hear you express your feelings towards how their behaviour made you feel, why are you apologizing for wanting to have your feelings to be validated? If you have information you need to share with them, why are you apologizing for taking up a portion of their time?

You deserve to hold space. Practise not saying sorry for useless things that you do not need to be sorry for. Practise only apologizing when your actions or words warrant the need for an apology to the other person. When someone bumps into you, say "excuse me". This little change in the words out of your mouth will feel uncomfortable at first, it will feel as though you are being rude. But you're not being rude, this phrase is a polite way to ask someone to move out of your way. That's right, they were in your way, so you need not apologize to them. Once you do this a few times, you'll feel something small inside you that resembles self-respect. This will grow the more times you do it, until one day it becomes normal. Normal for you to say excuse me when someone is in your way. Not sorry. Now take this up a level and begin to use it in your relationships at home, at work, and in the community. If someone says something or does something that affects you in a negative way, you deserve the space to bring it to their attention. Not sorry.

FOR THOSE THAT SHOULDERED MORE RESPONSIBILITY THAN THEY SHOULD HAVE HAD TO

Some people are born to take care of their parents and siblings without ever having agreed to the job. The natural progression of life is that once you become an adult, you separate from your parents and live a life independent of your family of origin. But, if you learn at a very young age that you are responsible for your parents and your siblings because they themselves are stuck in patterns of self-destruction, as you grew into adulthood, you most likely develop poor boundaries due to this lifelong relationship of codependence.

Codependence describes a relationship where one person with low self-esteem and a strong desire for approval has an unhealthy attachment to another, often controlling or manipulative, person. The guilt that comes from trying to form boundaries in your adult life after you have spent your younger years taking care of your parents and siblings is a confusing battle between your heart and your head. When you attempt to develop a boundary, the guilt and the shame you face from those affected is enough to send you down a spiral of self-loathing and self-criticism. You have never been good at saying no, but that changes today.

I give you guilt-free permission to draw a line around your body like you used to do when you were little, lying on the sand and being traced around. Let's bring the fun back and start drawing. OK, this process is not going to feel fun exactly, but hear me out when I say that the aftermath of the drawing will feel like a world without weight. If you keep the end goal in mind, the process will be fun in the same way that it is fun to train for a marathon. You will be fatigued and constantly needing to pull determination in order to keep going in the beginning, but once you get rolling, you will start to feel your body change and your health will start to improve. After you have adjusted to the training sessions, it becomes fun to watch and feel the transformation in both your body and your mind. For those that have never trained for a marathon, you may have experienced a similar process with another workout routine or after committing to a healthy eating plan. If you have never stuck out a process like this long enough to know what I'm talking about here, then you are about to have a massive transformation as you are about to start your training sessions right now!

My guilt-free permission is in line with my belief in the circle of life that God has set out for us. If you read *Boundaries* by

John Townsend and Henry Cloud, it talks about how to form proper boundaries in line with God's wishes. He describes how the Bible teaches that adults should take care of their elderly parents and give proper recognition to those that are really in need. However, the Bible also states that an adult with children and grandchildren should first take care of their own. The natural order of things does not say the adult must take care of their children and their parents and their siblings and their grandparents and their aunties and their uncles, all at the same time. Townsend and Cloud reassure that it is pleasing to God that an adult will first take care of their own family. This is the natural order in keeping thriving generations alive and strong.

It is good to feel grateful to our parents and to repay them for what they have given us, however this can easily start getting a little cloudy. Our parents and adult siblings may not actually be in need. They may instead just be irresponsible. Or, if they are actually in need, your boundaries may be so clouded that you may not be able to limit the time and energy you put into helping them until begins to dominate your life, taking care away from your actual family. This is when our marriages start to get into trouble and when our children's needs become neglected. Our families have emotional needs that must be met, or else new generations of insecurity, lack of self-worth, and no boundaries will form, and we will never change. Children will keep getting hurt and the cycle of debilitating mental health issues will continue, generation after generation. This stops with you, starting today. Clear boundaries that dictate what you are willing to give to your family of origin will allow you to continue to love and appreciate your parents and adult siblings without growing resentment for them. I know this because I have suffered from trying to fix people all my life. This is the kind of thing they don't teach you in school though, so how else would we know?

My parents came up to visit me one day while I was in college, and they took me out for dinner to Applebee's. It was the day my younger brother, Chris, got into his accident. My mom and dad sat across from me at the table and my older brother sat beside me. Chris had decided not to come with them that day, for whatever reason. I remember looking out the window that day and thinking, *This is how it's going to be from now on, just the four of us...* A cloud of sadness filled my heart as I sat in this random odd vision that had swept over me. I shook my head as if to shake out the crazy thought. After my parents left that afternoon, I couldn't shake that unsettling feeling. Two hours later, my dad phoned. They had gotten home to find out that my little brother was missing. They quickly found out that he had been in a quad accident down the road and the neighbour had called an ambulance. Soon after, STARS was called as they were not sure he was going to make it. I was eighteen years old and my life after that phone call was never the same.

I became the fixer in my broken family. I was called to help my distraught parents in the aftermath. Their drinking escalated substantially after the funeral was said and done, as their new reality without their baby boy wasn't anything they were willing to take on sober. The pain is surreal when you lose someone like that so fast. And fast or slow, any parent that loses their child is left with a huge hole in their heart that nothing can fill. Mine tried to fill theirs with vodka. A lot of vodka. Then came destruction, shame, violence, unthinkable actions, and more vodka, all poured into those deep, dark holes. It's interesting to watch, as those on the path of destruction have a marked pattern of behaviour, if you know how to detect it. I had no idea at that time though. I was just a young, hopeful girl that wanted to one day fix the hurt in the eyes of the people she loved so dearly. Like a ripple effect, everyone feels destruction as it spreads like wildfire. That's where it all began for me. I was made immediately responsible for protecting my beaten, broken mother; trying to simmer the anger in my father that I no longer recognized; and soothing my grandparents as they agonized over the loss of their grandchild, and a son they couldn't take the pain away from. My older brother kept quietly to himself over the years, burying all the pain he felt.

I spent years exhausting myself trying to fix everyone. If I wasn't spending my time trying to help them, I was dealt a nice hand of guilt that sat on my heart, which was always just enough to make me keep trying, even though it was slowly destroying me.

As we all find out eventually, I was about to learn that people do not change just because you want them to.

When my dad started beating my mother, I forced my brother to pick her up and put her in my car. I couldn't get her away safe any other way. I was nineteen. We waited until my dad had left for the grain truck that day and then we carried her out. I took us to a friend's house and we hid for a while. I left my job. We stayed hidden until we had a plan and felt safe enough to come out of hiding. I set my mother up at my auntie and uncle's. They lived on the farm where my mother had grown up. My uncle was my mom's older brother, and he had married a very strong Danish wife. They promised to keep her safe until we could trust my mom enough to stay away from my dad and start a life on her own. They were willing to stand in front of her while holding hunting rifles as my dad drove by. That's how bad it was. I left to try to start my own life. I empowered her every day until she was ready to move to town and start her own life. The cycle continued.

Along with that, my grandparents told me that if I didn't bring my son to see my dad, then he wouldn't stay sober. They told me it was my duty to bring my son to see him, and if I didn't,

I wasn't the daughter or granddaughter I should be. They had been so good to me all my life that I thought I had better go. It was destroying me, balancing all of these things, and it wasn't working. My dad drank anyway. My mom drank anyway.

Fast forward.

I tried to form boundaries with my parents and grandparents once I was married, had had my next two children, and was getting my nursing degree. I had called my grandpa to tell him that I could no longer keep going home to try and keep my dad sober. I told him it wasn't working and it was destroying me. I told him I wanted to focus on my children, be a good mom to them, and be a good wife to my husband that loved us. My grandpa was so upset with me that day. It all came from fear and pain, but he shamed me for giving up on my dad. He cried. He said I would have to live with my choice to give up on my dad, but that he would never give up on him like I had. All of that pain just breathed into my soul. I'll never forget the shame, and some days I still have to remind myself that I needed to do it to protect my sanity and my immediate family. I had young kids, I was trying to further my career, and I had to find a way to navigate a healthy marriage despite having no childhood teachings in that department. Making the choice to give up on my dad was hard enough, the shame and disappointment from my grandparent's didn't help. But everybody hurts.

In my mind, my parents didn't love me enough to stop drinking, and my grandparents didn't care about my wellbeing enough to let me stop trying to sober them up. My self-worth was fought for from the ground up. It has taken many self-talks and much inner guidance in meditation to believe that I am worthy of loving.

Fast forward.

DRAWING THE LINES

I have had to learn what physical, mental, and manipulative abuse look like, and now that I am aware, I make choices to protect my boundaries by focusing on love as my base. This takes a lot of work and perseverance, and I still get triggered. Like in the formation of any good habit, you have to work to keep from falling backward into old comforts. Old habits. For me, those old habits are allowing other people to treat me poorly, trying to fix people, and taking responsibility for other people's happiness.

I used to think I wasn't worth it. Now I've changed.

Why am I telling you all of this?

Because it's a never-ending story, and I had to learn that the hard way. I want to save you the pain of trying to figure it out on your own. You are worthy of setting boundaries to protect yourself from being responsible for other people's health and happiness. It is not up to you to make other people happy. It is up to you to find happiness in yourself and to care for whoever it is that fills your heart without emptying your bucket. Giving is good for the soul, so find a way to give to people that appreciate it.

WHAT BOUNDARIES LOOK LIKE

Let's now talk about what boundaries actually are. I like to think of them as property lines. If you are walking down a street, you don't go onto someone else's driveway and hit their truck, and you don't stop to play soccer on their lawn either. It is their property, not yours to use or abuse. Your body and your soul are your property, not to be stepped upon or into to be used or abused in any way. I'm talking physical and emotional boundaries here; you must learn how to set both so that people do not use you, take advantage of your kindness, hurt you, or intrude over your value system. Boundaries will become your lifeline, and your world will change once you create them and then continue to honour and respect them. So, let's figure out how to create them.

IDENTIFICATION

First, we must identify where our boundaries are needed. Anyone in your life that causes you to feel stress, guilt, shame, anger, or fear in a conversation or situation is crossing a boundary. After you figure out the emotion you are made to feel, pinpoint the situations where it is felt the worst. Then, identify why you feel this way and what would make the feeling dissipate. Think about what value this negative emotion of yours is attached to—the person or situation that is crossing your boundaries is crossing over one or more of the internal values you hold in your ethical system, which is why it makes you feel so uncomfortable. Once you figure this out, you have identified the boundary issue. This goes for all people in our lives—children, spouses, parents, family, friends, and strangers.

Example: What's the scariest word? The word that gives most people anxiety to say because they don't want to cause conflict or hurt another person's feelings if they use it? The most obvious boundary identification is when you just can't say *no*. You see it in stressed-out parents—they are afraid that by telling their kid no, their kid might not love them as much, they might rebel, they might be mad at them, or they might throw a tantrum. You see it in codependent people who are afraid to say no for fear that it may hurt the person they are emotionally attached to and feel responsible for, or that it may cause the person to have an adult tantrum, which turns peace into conflict again. Conflict is scary for most, I'd say. You see it in that sixteen-year-old girl that went to the party and was chosen by that boy from the hockey team that night; his big brown eyes could make her do anything when he looked at her like that. He made her feel special, better than the rest somehow. But as she lay there after, after not saying no, she felt the tears fill her eyes. He had just gotten up and left to go back to the party. Suddenly she remembered just how worthless she really was; funny she almost fell for it—almost thought she was worth something more.

> *Boundary identification:* Fear of saying the word no.
>
> *Boundary conflict:* When others have a lack of respect for you and take advantage of you to meet their own selfish needs.
>
> *Values being crossed:* Respect and integrity.

CREATION

Second comes creation. Once you have established that you have a negative emotion that has crossed something in your value system, you must plan to form a much-needed boundary.

First in the plan is to respond, not react. If you react, you have let the person crossing your boundary have power over you. You must keep power over yourself and keep in control, so keep your emotions at bay and figure out how to respond rather than react.

How do I do this? I practice it *a lot*. My emotions start rising when my triggers are set off. My past flashes back into my present self and I almost lose control of my emotions. This is when I go for a run if I can, take deep breaths in the bathroom if that's the only escape I can conjure, and self-talk myself back into control. It is not easy and you won't be perfect at it. Your ability to do it will also be directly affected by how much sleep you have had, your hormone cycle, your tolerance level, your diet, and your mental state at the time. It is very important in the creation process though—remember to respond rather than react. Responding allows you to find the calm and time you need to explain why you no longer accept whatever boundary-conflicting behaviour the person has engaged in and why your boundary is important to you. The thing about honesty is, nobody can argue with it.

To create the boundary: figure out what it is that is causing you to be upset, understand what it is you would like to change, plan how you are going to communicate it with the person you require changes with.

Example 1: When you talk over me, it makes me feel frustrated and belittled. When you overpower me in conversations, it causes me to shut down and bottle up my emotions. When you interrupt me, I feel unable to express my needs. I will no longer accept this unhealthy communication pattern with you. If you are unwilling to let me speak, I will not partake in the conversation.

DRAWING THE LINES

Boundary conflict: When others hinder my ability to properly communicate because they lack consideration for my needs and emotions.

Values being crossed: Respect, love, and understanding.

Boundary creation: Healthy communication requires both parties having the opportunity to express their emotions and respectfully engage in finding a solution. Your feelings matter just as much as the person with whom you are in conversation with. It is up to you to be honest about the way you feel when you are attempting to resolve a conflict. If the other person will not agree to let you speak, the conversation becomes one sided and you have the ability to choose to exit the conversation.

Example 2: When you drink you are mean. I will no longer accept this treatment from you. If you are going to drink, I choose to not be around you.

Boundary conflict: When others mistreat me.

Values being crossed: Love, respect, and kindness.

Boundary creation: You have no control over what other people choose to do, but you do have control over what you are willing to accept. By stating that you will no longer be around this person when they are drunk leaves the choice in their hands. If they continue to drink around you, you can now remove yourself from this person, guilt-free, knowing that they have made the choice. It's not up to you to choose the outcome, but it is absolutely up to you to be honest with yourself and with the person involved about how they make you feel and the boundary you will no longer allow them to cross.

PRACTISE

Practise makes progress. The hardest part is over, but you must now practise enforcing your boundaries in order to develop this new skill. If you are new to setting boundaries, you must start by avoiding anyone that has intimidated you in the past or anyone that has the ability to trigger your past wounds and set you into your old cycle of acceptance. Practise instead on people that do not have a direct relation to you until you feel more confident in your ability to take your assertive action to those that know how to hurt you.

Give yourself much grace as it will take a lot of practise to gain confidence in this process and it will hurt like you never expected. Sometimes the outcome won't be what you hoped it would be, but when that happens, you must make an absolute promise to yourself to continue to hold your boundaries and not give in. The only way you can build trust in yourself is to never break this promise when someone hurts you.

Going forth, you must always protect your vulnerable inner child, for that little person from your past still lives within you and is still scared and alone. Learn to set boundaries for others and yourself. It will be what separates hard from easy, and life will start making a lot more sense for you afterward. Love people where they are at, and focus on you.

Honesty plus courage equals freedom.

> *"If you don't like something, change it.*
> *If you can't change it,*
> *change your attitude."*
>
> — Maya Angelou

21.
A LITTLE PERSPECTIVE

As you may remember, there are two things in this life that will change your whole world in a matter of seconds. The first was boundaries. The second is perspective.

Perspective is the key to a whole new life, simply by manipulating your ego and resetting the way your mind views the world. Are you going to let other people dictate what you can and should do with your life? I didn't think so.

Let me remind you of the proximity principle: the people you surround yourself with the most are who you are going to become. So, here's the thing: if you hang around lazy people, you will become lazier than if you were to hang around people who are on the move. Movers and shakers attract more movers and shakers. If the people around you are telling you that your dream is crazy, get away from them. If they talk about other people's success with judgment, keep your distance. It is these kinds of people that do not want others to succeed and project their own unhappiness, fear, and discontentment onto them.

The thing about life is that it can be whatever you want it to be, just by looking at it through a different lens. Those that sit in discontentment can sulk and blame others (the government, their parents, their kids, their bosses) for their problems. Those that love watching the news and believe that the world is ending can live their lives with resentment toward what they believe is happening around them. Those that live their lives with the understanding that mistrust is indeed all around us can choose to stay grateful, logical, and optimistic and live full and happy lives. Those that work their asses off to achieve whatever goal or dream they set out to achieve can live life in another realm of happiness and contentment. It is these last couple of folks that have found true freedom in their souls. That's the kind of stuff Maslow was talking about in his brilliant pyramid of human needs: the point where you find self-actualization. So, what lens will you choose to look at life through? And what people will you surround yourself with so that you can fully live this life?

Now let's explore a new perspective with which you can look at yourself. Let's play a little game. We'll call it a confidence experiment. I want you to start silently studying people and listening to what your intuition tells you about their character. Pay attention to what you see through your own lens, as informed by your own life experiences. Notice things about people that others don't seem to notice. You might doubt yourself and think you may be wrong about a certain person, but deep down, you know better. Don't say a word to anyone about this experiment. Let time pass

A LITTLE PERSPECTIVE

by and watch what happens. The person you once noticed will eventually start showing their true character and other people will start to notice. Soon you will hear people speak their disbelief about what that person did or said. Funny thing for you is, you knew their character all along. Check mark.

Start to trust your instincts. I can promise you that the majority of people around you don't bother to take the time to listen to their instincts or even open themselves up enough to learn about them. How did you find out about your instincts? They just happened to show up, didn't they? Because you were seeking something more, praying for something deeper. Trusting your instincts is a strength that very few in the world actually possess, and with it, you can go far. You can gain an understanding that some never get the chance to gain.

Never stop seeking knowledge and using what you learn. You'll be shocked at how your life shifts, amazed at the unfathomed awareness you gain. This is where your life starts to transform. Be patient now, for nothing big happens overnight. Just start to play the game and pay attention to the way it shifts your life and the confidence that comes with changing the people you surround yourself with.

It will be confusing at times when you start to outgrow certain people you have loved in your life. It will almost be like you are surpassing them in a spiritual sense, finding yourself in a new chapter of your life where you are not sure if you and them fit together. It's uncomfortable, but be patient. Sit in the feeling for a while, but keep forging ahead with the values and goals at the forefront of your path. Fill your path with people that fill your soul rather than deplete it. Go in peace down this path while keeping silent about who your new-found, elevated spirit is evolving into, for people won't understand when you try to tell them. Just smile, love them all where they are, and keep going.

Change your lens. Be grateful and humble. Hold the power of your strength with what you intuitively understand and don't say a word about it, just keep on cruising your path to a life full of freedom and the opportunity for everlasting change.

THE POWER OF YOUR MIND

Perspective is all about mind work. When you go through life, you absorb everything around you and your normal becomes how you think. If you have ever read studies on the mind or read about what certain people have accomplished, you can better understand that the mind creates limits, and until you learn how to gain true access to the power of your mind, you will be held hostage by those limits so that everything outside of them seems impossible. Let me explain. Back to nursing class we go.

Sigmund Freud, a famous neurologist known for his theories on psychoanalysis, was a major contributor to the evolution of the study of the human mind. He studied different segments and intricacies of the conscious and subconscious makeup of the human brain and introduced what is known as the Freudian principles. Because you didn't sign up to join a psychology class today, I'll sum these up in a just a few short parts to give you a better understanding of how studies in science are once again linked to the invisible parts of what makes us who we are. The tough part about this topic however, is because our subconscious is invisible, it is difficult to provide evidence-based practise on his theories. This is why so much of his work became famous through observational studies of individual experiences going through psychoanalysis modes of treatment.

The id, ego, and superego Freud described are basically the psyche in three parts. The id is the primitive, instinctual part of our mental function in which we have basic urges to meet needs.

A LITTLE PERSPECTIVE

A newborn's mental function is all id, as when we enter this world, we move through all actions with these basic instincts for survival. This part of our psyche is not affected by logic. It's part of our innate knowing and used to meet our basic needs. The ego is our conscious mind, which is completely affected by the external world around us. The ego works by thinking, making decisions, and employing logic, and it is what we think of ourselves to be. The superego is our moral compass, which develops when we reach the age of four or five. It is designed to control the impulses of the id, and it is within this section of our psyche that we hold our morals.

The purpose of this little psychology lesson is simply to show you that your psyche has different parts that you may not be aware of, and this model has been studied for years and used as a basis for treatment for numerous mental health issues. It is through continued study of this model that scientists have found diagnosable disorders such as post-traumatic stress disorder and many others linked to hidden memories—those memories that affect us even while we are unaware of them.

This information about your psyche is imperative as you begin to work through the layers of your inner self and start living in a more conscious state where you can better understand why you feel the emotions and make the decisions you do. Therapy works wonders for unpacking these hidden answers within us. Or, if you choose to continue to work independently on your healing, you can turn inward, meditate, and pray. Remember, wherever you put your energy is where it will make things grow. If you put your energy into meditation in order to learn how to communicate with your soul, then you will start to find the answers. Look to those with specialized knowledge in these areas to gain practise techniques to help you break through. Eckhart Tolle and Gabby Bernstein are options to research if you need a place to start with meditation. For now, let's dive a little deeper into the id, ego, and superego.

THE ID

Remember Maslow's pyramid? The id part of the brain is what allows us to meet our basic needs, and the simplicity of our human survival instincts can be linked to much of our behaviour and the decisions we make. The most important thing to remember about this part of the psyche is that we must be wary of impulsive actions without logic. The id will fight for our survival when we are in serious danger, but in everyday happenings, if the superego doesn't intervene, the id can get us in trouble. We need to think about why we want to do things before we do them. Enough said.

THE EGO

When I talk about the ego, I am referring to the part of the psyche that creates our own idea of ourselves and our limitations. Imposter syndrome lives here. With imposter syndrome, you don't believe you are capable or qualified in a certain area of your life, despite having succeeded or achieved in that area. There are five specific parts to imposter syndrome, but in summary, it includes not feeling like an expert and striving for perfection. If you don't get something right the first time, you may feel like you are not qualified to do that thing. Or, you may believe that you must know everything about a particular subject or that you must reach a certain title before you can call yourself an expert; anything less and you question your competence. This happens to each of us along the stages of achievement. You may have experienced it while moving into a new career title, becoming a parent, or changing your personality from being a people pleaser to a more confident, assertive leader. It is within the ego that we feel we need pride in order to feel good about ourselves. Where we feel we need to achieve certain things to be worthy.

It's time to put that ego in check. It is the ego that engages in the comparison game, makes you think you need to be more like someone else, and will lead you astray from the true form of who you are in your soul. Your ego needs material things or constant achievements to make you feel worthy, but it is what drives you to become something more. The most important takeaway you need to understand is that you have the ability to completely control your ego. It is your logical thoughts and decision maker. When you listen to yourself, you will hear your ego first. It sounds like the mean person telling you that you are not good enough. When you quiet the ego, you will begin to hear your soul come through. It is within the wiser self of your soul that you will find answers that bring you peace in who you really are and what you actually need to feel fulfilled. Controlling your ego is a daily practice that you will feel overwhelmed by at first. But, once you start, you'll understand exactly what I'm talking about.

As I mentioned, there are limitations within our egos, so to change your limitations, you need to change your perspective. This is how it all ties in. When you change your thinking, you change your expectation of normal, you change what you feel you are capable of, and you change the way you care about what other people think of you. Removing fear of judgment opens up a million new doors. You will have the ability to kick out any bad thoughts that pass through your brain. You will have this ability if you start commanding your ego, rather than allowing your ego to command you.

Our mind's eye is what we believe to be true. It is the movie we play in our heads, and it can cause anxiety, even when we are just imagining things happening. Do yourself a favour and research "The Work" by Byron Katie. It is a process through which she talks about freedom from suffering and has you answer four questions in order to help you see what is troubling you in a different light. It's all about finding answers from the inside and opening your mind to life-changing insights. Honestly, this woman is brilliant. Any time you change your perspective, you change your life. And it really does only take minutes.

If you want more work on limitations with regards to the ego, your self-reflection time is about to get a whole lot more interesting. Contemplating stories of other people's achievements and experiences can help you see past what your ego considers to be your normal. You can read about the terrible suffering endured through the Holocaust or the story of Nelson Mandela to help you see what other people are capable of surviving. You can hear many other stories of survival on Oprah Winfrey's *Super Soul Sunday* podcast, as well as from people like David Goggins, who is becoming a huge influencer when it comes to the capabilities of the human body through his experience with eliminating limitations. I love listening to people's stories. I find them fascinating, and quite often it helps me to change my perspective of how I look at my own experiences and limitations. Those that seek to gain knowledge and growth hold an open mind to the study of people.

THE SUPEREGO

The superego is said to be an extended part of your ego. It is where your moral compass lives, and in Freudian principles, it is where your self-criticism comes from. When we look at the unique cultures of this world, our morals and values vary greatly based on religion, poverty, historical cultural belief systems, and family generational values. What we learn forms our value and belief systems. However, I believe our moral compass is built inside of us as an innate act of the higher power in original creation. We just have to be able to connect with our souls to hear it. For those born into a culture where normal includes hurting other people, it becomes generational to pass that belief of normal on. I have to argue though, that anyone who hurts another being must at some point feel a sense of sadness or remorse. This is a topic that holds many layers with many variables affecting each situation, but to simplify it here, just know that your value system can be readjusted as you set new expectations for your ego.

RESET YOUR THERMOSTAT

If there is one thing about perspective that will change how much you suffer, how grateful you are, and how you enjoy your life, it is resetting your belief system. I've heard many people discuss different versions of how to visualize resetting your limitations and beliefs about yourself in order to initiate true change, but the one that resonates most with me is changing your thermostat. In science, we discuss that our bodies grow accustomed to certain comfort levels. These comforts can be safe homes with loving families or jobs we know so well that we can do them on autopilot without giving much thought to the process. Some of us have been subjected to a lot of drama in our lives, so, surprisingly enough, drama or hurt can become a comfort, and when we are not in the stress response, our bodies can begin to crave it—to return back to our normal. This in particular is the cycle of abuse, or the girl that keeps choosing mean boys, or the person you know that spends their time seeking out constant drama. It is an unconscious desire we need to be made aware of.

The idea behind the thermostat is that just as how you can change a thermostat's settings to adjust the temperature in a room, so you can change your own settings for things you want to change in your life. For example, if you normally set your thermostat to nineteen degrees, the house will heat or cool to nineteen degrees. If you set your internal thermostat to always accept maltreatment to the point of you feeling down, you will adjust to the comfort of feeling down due to the external influences around you. Your setting is at victim mentality. Change that thermostat to read strong and firm in the way people treat you, and soon you will adjust to a new feeling of comfort where you are able to hold people accountable for the way they treat you. You can use this analogy for anything you want to change, from how you envision your body to look, to your career achievements. Just envision yourself how you would be after the change. This focus begins to form a new thought pattern in you, which in turn changes your behaviour, which develops into a newly formed vision. After a while, this new vision becomes your new comfort.

IMPOSTER SYNDROME

So, a little about imposter syndrome. If you have never heard of this term before, it's when a person doubts their skills or accomplishments and has an internal fear of being found out that they are not an expert. They may wonder if they are even capable in their position of authority, or they believe they must be the hardest worker, reach the highest level of achievement, or know all of the answers in a particular area, in order to not be a fraud. This was me for most of my nursing career. Tell me I'm not the only one that has felt this: you get out of your comfort zone and think to yourself, *Who do you think you are?* The negative self-talk rolls in. Well, only you can change that, and faking it until you make it sometimes is the only way.

Not all of us can know everything about everything, so practise showing confidence in what you do know, and be honest about what you don't know without any embarrassment for not knowing or for feeling like you should know. We are all human! And believe it or not, we all feel the same way at different times in our lives.

The problem with people is our egos, and the fact that we feel we have to hide our feelings to make it look to others like we are not vulnerable, don't make mistakes, or know everything in order to save face and look more amazing than the next person. We need to stop this. We all have strengths in different areas. Figure out what yours are and work with them to find your passion or your purpose. Take what you are mediocre at and understand that you cannot be the best at everything. All you can do is give yourself grace in knowing we are all here, doing our best, with the knowledge and the ability we have. Once you truly believe this, you will feel a huge pressure lift off your shoulders, and you can start to allow yourself the permission to get out of the rat race.

VICTIM MENTALITY

Stop being the victim. That's it. The things that happen to you can be really hard, but in every experience, there is a lesson, so hold yourself accountable for how you could have done things differently and move forward. Do not blame others for your struggles, because although they may be the original cause, it is up to you to change the outcome of who you are becoming.

Victims do not change. They do not grow. Victims spend their lives living in the past, full of resentment and regret. When you reach the point in your life where you get to look back, you do not want to spend that time wishing you would have done things differently.

Forgive yourself for your past choices, which were based only on what you knew at the time, and allow yourself the grace to carry forward toward change.

Don't wait to change the things you need to change in order to find happiness. Reflect on what you want to change about yourself and get to work. Be honest, even though you won't like it.

As you move into these next steps of change, you must also move into the next most important thing besides perspective that will allow the past to be left behind you. Forgiveness.

FORGIVENESS, THE FREEDOM OF SOUL

In *The Book of Joy*, Desmond Tutu and the Dalai Lama discuss the importance of forgiveness as a powerful practice in breaking the cycle of suffering. Rather than responding to harm by causing more harm or allowing resentment or anger to deteriorate you, you can choose to forgive and allow room for compassion. Desmond Tutu and the Dalai Lama explain that forgiveness requires you to distinguish between the person and their action. Forgiveness is not the same as condoning a harmful action, and it takes much strength to look beyond an action and see the person who committed it as a separate entity.

In practice, this means not being mad at the alcoholic, but being mad at the choice they made to consume and become addicted to alcohol. It means not being mad at the person that caused you pain, but being mad at the actions the person took to cause you that pain.

The ones that hurt other people have no ability to heal themselves, and so they continue the cycle. It's like the pain inside them is leaking out of them. If anything, you should feel sorry for them, because the shame they feel inside is something they have to live with, and they most likely will never be strong enough to stop the toxic pattern of their behaviour. They will never get to live true to their souls, and that is really sad.

Compassion is a damn tricky thing, and it is far easier said than done, I can promise you that. But I can also promise you that once you develop the ability to forgive, you will also be giving yourself an everlasting freedom from toxic emotions that can cause damage to you. The other freedom forgiveness provides is a release of the power a person holds over you to affect your emotions and behaviours. Once you are able to let anger go, people can no longer hold that power over you. This is imperative in becoming completely independent.

Think of forgiving like setting your pain free. When you allow someone to keep you in a state of hurt and anger, you are allowing them to control you. The thing I have preached about the most in this book is how important it is to gain complete control of your life and to become solely dependent on yourself. To not allow others to dictate how your life will go. You have to set the pain you feel from others that have hurt you, free so that you can heal. Locked pain and buried resentment are poisons inside of you. They are toxic and they will find a way to surface through mental and physical ailments. You can't keep them buried forever.

My favourite part about forgiveness is the feeling of peace after you do it. It literally feels like a huge weight lifted off your shoulders and your chest. It really is freedom. My other favourite part is that even when you can forgive, it does not mean you ever forget. Once others lose your trust, they can consider it gone. Second chances are one thing, but they come knowing that you both know what they were once capable of. You'll always be fine though, so this makes it easier for you to sleep at night.

Letting go feels scary and lonely, but sometimes we have no choice. Sometimes you just have to hold what you have and move forward.

You're going to get better at letting go.

Letting go comes with a process of healing that I should prepare you for. It took the death of my father to shock me into confronting my toxic shit storm, and yours will show up one day too. Be ready when it does, as your fate depends on it. For me, it felt like a hurricane of emotions I had no idea I was even holding on to. Memories and emotions from years ago surfaced: how scared and lost I had felt as a girl and how guilty I had felt when I stepped back from providing care for my dad. Like staring the truth in the face, I could no longer ignore these things. I had to look my demons straight in the eye. The aftermath felt like a freedom I couldn't have imagined before. It's crazy that we can trudge through hard times with our shoulders back and heads held strong. We keep going. Adrenaline pushes us through almost anything. But we know we are in real trouble when we can talk about the awful things we have felt without a waver in our voices or the shed of a tear. Like it were just another day.

I remember the look on my best friend's face when I told her about the most awful things I had gone through. I saw astonishment and worry in her eyes. She had never been so quiet in all our thirty-five years of friendship. The way I talked about my memories was without regard for how much pain it caused. It was without consideration for how unacceptable it was for me to have endured as a young girl. Today, I don't tell the same stories in that same way that I used to. Now, I am able to talk about it with regard to how it actually affected me, because I finally let myself feel all the pain. When you are healed, you will find you are able to discuss past hurt with consideration for the pain you felt, but not spiral back into that pain. You can acknowledge the empathy for your past self that endured the hurt, and not hide from the fact that it affected you. You no longer talk in a state of denial for your past. You are no longer disassociated from your soul. Acceptance is a form of freedom. You develop a deeper love for yourself, all by letting it go.

When you are faced with a decision to forgive or not, remember that every person came into this world as an innocent child. Think of the person who has done wrong as the young boy or girl they once were. Picture their sandy blond hair or their dark brown eyes, their little arms and hands, their little legs and feet that carry them. Think about them running and playing, living a life that was good for them, that is until at some point when someone hurt them. Don't take what they did to you personally anymore. They didn't mean to cause you hurt. They simply projected the hurt they had buried inside of themselves that had turned into a toxic poison that eventually ate through their soul. They became a product of their environment. How do you think killers are born? Little kids don't desire to hurt unless someone shows them how. Unless someone shows them why.

Be mad at the alcohol, not the man that suffers from an addiction to it. Be mad at the drugs, not the woman that can't live without the high. Be mad at the life that caused their hurt to be so painful that they lost the fight. Feel sorry for them because they can't be saved. But save yourself. It's the only thing you can do and it's the only thing that matters. Once you are free, fly away.

"Calmness is the cradle of power."
— Josiah Gilbert Holland

22.

SUPERPOWERS

Before we talk about superpowers, I have to tell you that I had my baby! I woke up the other morning and felt a little leak happening, saw my doctor for an appointment, and carried on with my day as per usual. I had some lunch with a few friends and then I calmly headed home to let my husband know it was time.

I'll tell you what, those fourth ones just kind of slip right on out of there.

Now, here I am with the cuddles, new love, spit up, and sleepless nights. I was carrying this little angel when I started writing this book. She's a beautiful little girl, and we named her Ayla. All three of my babies were overdue, but this little peach decided to come three weeks early and showed up on December 31, ending 2022 in the most special way. My heart is very full.

The high I used to get from heartache and stress has been replaced with a different high, one that I now get when something amazing happens in life, like new love. This is my hope for you, to ride high on life, but you can't ride high on life if you are riding high on stress.

There is something so addicting about riding an adrenaline high, and like any addiction, your body adjusts. You do it. Then you just keep doing it. Then years pass by, and you realize that now it's all you know. I will keep fighting for all of you riding the high of duress to replace it with the high of the sweetest joy and the purest love, because no one in this life deserves any less than that.

Let me take you back to nursing school for a minute, because I know you all love it when I teach you nursing stuff you didn't ask to be taught. Hear me out. Time doesn't heal wounds completely, but if given the chance, it dulls the severity substantially. Let's walk through how your physical body processes wounds, like a deep cut through the flesh, because if you look closely, it mimics the emotional grieving process that is required to heal emotional wounds of the heart. When your skin is injured, your body sets into motion a series of events called the cascade of healing in order to repair your wound.

The four phases of wound healing are the homeostasis phase, inflammatory phase, proliferative phase, and maturation phase.

1. *The homeostasis phase.* This is the first phase which begins with the onset of injury. It sends out the call for emergency repair and initiates the clotting system, which stops the bleeding.

    This is your shock phase. Like when that phone call came in. Like when your world changed.

> Adrenaline rush
> The world stops; your heart bleeds
> Shock for survival

2. *The inflammatory phase.* The focus here is to destroy bacteria and debris to prepare the wound bed for the growth of new tissue. Immune system cells are called in for action. There is redness and swelling... This phase hurts.

> Your world has changed
> This pain is surreal; throbbing
> This hurt will not stop

3. *The proliferative phase.* This is the phase of new tissue growth, when the body fills and covers the wound—a process called epithelialization.

> The light starts to show
> Throbbing settles; pain is real
> A new way of life

4. *The maturation phase.* In this phase, the new tissue grows stronger. Collagen fibres reorganize and the tissue remodels and matures. Its tensile strength increases, but it will never surpass 80% of the strength it used to be.

> Scar tissue at best
> Time helps the severity
> I can survive this

You see, the healing process is complex, but remarkable. The thing is, in the physical cascade of healing, there are variables that can interrupt or hinder the process such as moisture, infection, maceration, malnutrition, reinjury, and other disease factors. Our emotional healing process can be hindered by variables too. Denial, a continued pattern of emotional reinjury, numbing through substance abuse, sleep deprivation, isolation, and lack of self-worth, to name a few. Like I've said earlier, our physical and emotional selves are connected. God built in us the patterns of process. So, if you know a little more about our physical processes, then you can start to connect that knowledge to our emotional processes and have some guidance on navigating wellness in all aspects.

But what does this all have to do with superpowers?

It has to do with superpowers because you will only be able to find your superpower when you are at your best. To be at your best, you must heal all physical and emotional wounds. Now remember, 80% post-injury strength is about the best you will get, so this is important to remember when we start coming across triggers for old wounds in our lives. Learn to use your superpower to fend off these triggers, but be careful as old wounds are more sensitive to becoming reinjured.

I've watched *Wonder Woman* so many times. You know the one with Gal Gadot and Chris Pine? Such a classic movie about power and strength with a love story that everyone wishes they could feel. And Gal Gadot is such a good actress for her character! I just love how passionate and humble she is. And she's so beautiful! The other trait you will notice when you watch her is how calm she is under duress. And that is what I want to talk to you about superpowers for. To tell you that the greatest superpower you possess isn't always what you would expect.

Once you realize that you can overcome life's battle scenes with the proper attitude and armour, you will be able to move through the hard stuff with more tenacity, confidence, and grace. Your superpowers will allow you to handle triggers like Wonder Woman handles those gunmen on no man's land. Seriously, watch the movie, or at least the scene, so you understand what I'm talking about. You can mock the visuals all you want, or you can get over it and try it yourself—picture yourself blocking your triggers like Gadot blocks shots in the scene. Beauty emanates from a powerful human. Can you honestly tell me you haven't watched Chris Hemsworth as Thor and let your mind wander a bit to what it would be like to date him? Thor is sexy. Power is sexy. But power comes from knowing your inner strength and using it when you need to.

Superpowers that allow you to handle battles on your own and learn to not rely on anyone else to help you or change things for you are as follows:

- Emotional regulation
- Calm
- Grace
- Forgiveness (but not forgetting)
- Tenacity
- Resilience
- Compassion
- Tough skin
- Perseverance
- Honesty

So, what's your superpower?

I like to think that my superpower is calm. If you can stay calm in high-stress situations, amidst someone else losing it in front of you, when your children cause you to enter the red zone routinely, or when life hands you a first-hand lesson on heartache, then you can get through anything.

Find these superpowers within yourself and call them what they are, because not a lot of people possess them, especially not all of them. You though, can possess them all.

FIND WHAT'S HOLDING YOU BACK

By now, you will have determined that you are in need of a change, and deep inside, you know what you want. You have read my words and heard my nursing advice on the health and wellness you can achieve to feel your best, but now it's time to work on setting your dreams in motion in order to achieve a higher level of living. This process starts with first figuring out what to eliminate.

When we receive a patient into the emergency department, we must first rule things out in order to properly diagnose the main cause of the exhibiting signs and symptoms. This process involves assessments, labs, and CT or X-ray scans. We must eliminate the differentials before we can move forward in treating the underlying cause.

The process of elimination to find out what is holding you back in your psychological world is much the same. The assessment and examination process will look at a few things. The first is mindset. With what lens are you viewing your future? Optimistic and grateful, full of dreams and goals for your present and future self? Or pessimistic and entitled, full of resentment and blame for your present and future self? I hope for your sake it is not the latter. Your mindset matters in finding the life you seek, so eliminate negative self-talk and fear-based stagnation. It's holding you back.

Second, we look at people. This is an assessment and evaluation of who is holding you back. All of those that tell you that you can't. All of those that tell you that you're crazy to think you can have what you want. All of those that judge the success you already have. All of those that believe in compliancy, that things just are the way they are. All of those that disrespect you. All of those that hurt you. Eliminate them. They are holding you back.

Now consider your greatest strengths or superpowers. What superpower of yours is holding you back? This is something you are truly good at that still manages to hold you back. Mine is compassion. I innately always see the good in people, but it causes me to make excuses for their behaviour. Or, sometimes I find that my compassion causes me to lower my expectations of people because I can understand why they may have chosen to do or say the mean things they did or said. Sometimes, you just have to call people out on their bullshit and expect more from them. I do still get torn on this though. In my very first year of nursing school, my instructor told us to always remember that not all people are capable of the things you expect from them, and she encouraged us to meet people where they were. She reminded us that the world is full of all kinds of people with different abilities and strengths, and that what one person can do, another may not have in them. She ended up giving me some research assignments on patients with histories of alcoholism to help me learn how our body systems become physically dependent on alcohol and how it is not always mind over matter for some to beat addiction. What is your stance on this subject? Are all people capable of change if they are strong enough and open enough to learn? Do all people have the innate ability to conquer their demons because we all have souls inside us? I want to say yes to these questions so that I can hold people accountable for their actions, but my gut tells me that my instructor was right about these things. Not all people are cut from the same cloth, nor are they all capable of overcoming. But here's to trying, and to controlling the superpower that may be holding you back. So, what is it? Maybe it's patience turned laziness or confidence turned cockiness. Whatever it is, figure out how it's holding you back. Then, use it wisely, be aware of its power, and fly.

The last important part of developing your superpowers is about how you lead with them. To be humble is to not stand on top of a mountain looking down at all the people that do not possess the same strength and perseverance you had in making a necessary change. To be humble looks like having compassion without judgment. You can be very proud of who you are and what you have accomplished, but you can keep that feeling and just allow it to glow through the person you have become. I like to keep my true strength a little hidden from the world, because my superpowers are mine, and mine alone. I use them like weapons when I move through new challenges. I worked damn hard to strengthen them, and so I keep them within my soul.

"Where there is no struggle, there is no strength."
— Oprah Winfrey

23.

IT'S YOUR TURN

This book is a lot. It's about little pieces of the whole pie. It's all the parts that you need to make yourself whole, and with all of that comes a feeling of overwhelm. *Where do I even start?*

Start in the area where you most feel you need to change, then tackle each subsequent area as you progress. As you keep working, the compound effect will have you looking a lot different in the mirror. Once you understand that you have yourself to rely on and that you can look at who you are with love and accept your intricacies for what they are, then you can start to build your tribe. This tribe of people will walk with you and build you up, just as you will do for many others. This is the beginning of the rest of your life.

You have the permission to feel. This is the new you. Stop burying yourself in busy. Busy feels so good because it leaves no time to let thoughts and emotions come in. It is far easier to work longer hours, pick up shifts, run the kids to extra sports, reorganize your house, clean and tidy whatever room you walk into, run errands, and plan the next thing than it is to work on yourself. To take on the task of actual change is going to require you to pause the busy and allow your thoughts and emotions to surface.

Think of it like cleaning out clutter. It's tedious! It takes a lot of time. But when it's done, the house looks so much less busy, the room looks like it has its shit together, and everything has a place. It is the same inside of us! We must take the time to do the tedious deep cleaning. The most effective way to clean out crap is to take out all the crap, get rid of what you don't want or need, and keep the things that are necessary for daily life and the things that bring you feelings of happiness. Then, organize everything you're keeping so that everything has its place.

Do you know why we feel so good when we reorganize and deep clean? Because it makes us feel like we have our shit together. Like we have intention and peace and calm and time. If you know how good it feels to complete a task in your external environment, imagine how amazing it feels to deep clean and get rid of the crap in your internal environment. You won't understand until you do it. Trust me on this. It's going to change your life. Once you have begun the work, I want to hear your stories of progress and change.

In nursing school, we were not allowed to use the word "normal," but I use it in recognition of anyone living without daily doses of anger and pain inflicted upon them. Children deserve this. Adults deserve this. Everyone deserves to feel safe. I will never stop fighting for this. It's so damn basic, and yet people just don't understand it. You hear all these awful stories and you wonder how anyone can be crazy enough to have done such things to other people? Well, it starts with the little seeds that are planted inside of each and every one of us. These seeds grow, so we must pick our plants carefully.

I have spent much of my life in such privacy, ashamed of the things that have happened to me. When you realize you were not born into a normal way of living, it becomes something you want to hide. There is a lot of shame in a life of pain and destruction. You eventually look for normal—people who are not enduring toxic crap on a daily basis (that you know of). I remember feeling so safe and happy when I was hanging out with friends who had successful jobs and warm hearts. They were like an escape for me, like a vacation. I still feel the same today, but I have created my own happy bubble within my family unit in my safe home full of warm hearts and forgiving souls. It's not perfect, but it's normal. Everyone is safe, we are grateful, and we teach strong values to root, because children deserve the chance to have happy lives.

Create your own safe bubble within the boundary lines you set. Think of this like your house with a protective ring around it, or an island you live on that requires others to cross a bridge or board a boat in order to enter your world. Be very particular about who gets the privilege of entering your world. Your safe bubble. Where life is normal as I described: without anger toward or pain used against others. Without a doubt, pain will still come into your life, because that's life, but pain can be endured and you can be nurtured through pain when safety and love are at the forefront. You deserve this. Your children deserve this. You have the strength and the power to hold this.

When we can hold space for one another and know that we are not alone, we can begin to feel more comfortable with vulnerability. Vulnerability is going to become another one of your superpowers, because without it, we live coldly. We bury ourselves in busy, ignore our emotions, and never love ourselves enough to allow true happiness and peace to be a part of our daily lives. With vulnerability, you won't live like that anymore. Through whatever you are battling or whatever you wish to change, whatever you desire to have, you will find.

This is a reminder to understand your natural abilities and to make the necessary changes to harvest trust in yourself. The thing I want you to truly understand is that you have what it takes to take care of yourself and live the life you want. Once you feel this stir inside you, it will all start to fall into place—as long as you are willing to do the work. Don't give up and don't ever settle for less than you deserve. It's time to initiate the action, grieve the person you once were, and look forward to the person you will soon become. Trust yourself and change your life. For what it's worth, it will all be worthwhile.

~D

Printed in Canada